REBUILDING YOUR LIFE AFTER DOMESTIC VIOLENCE

STORIES OF STRENGTH AND SUCCESS

COMPILED BY
KC ANDREWS

Copyright © Broken to Brilliant™

The moral right of the authors has been asserted.

First published in Australia in 2018
by Broken to Brilliant Ltd™, Brisbane, Australia

ISBN

Paperback: 978-0-9945714-9-6

Epub: 978-0-9945714-8-9

Mobi: 978-0-9945714-7-2

All rights reserved. No part of this book may be reproduced or transmitted by any person or entity (including Google, Amazon or similar organisations), in any form or by any means, electronic or mechanical, including photocopying, recording, scanning or by any information storage and retrieval system, without prior permission in writing from the publisher.

Editor: Belinda Pollard
Proofreader: Alix Kwan
Cover image copyright © Petar Paunchev

A catalogue record for this book is available from the National Library of Australia

PRAISE FOR *TERROR TO TRIUMPH*

The stories in *Terror to Triumph* are honest, deeply personal and gut-wrenching. They are stories of absolute courage, heartfelt determination and indomitable spirit. The writers have overcome so much to reclaim their freedom and their lives. All of them have developed incredible strategies for survival and healing that they share with the reader. I salute you all and consider it a privilege and an honour to have joined you in the workshop weekend as you unpacked your stories and your incredible bravery. This book is triumphant, and a must read!
Fiona Ware, women's advocate, facilitator and children's author

Powerful, raw, unrestricted, brilliant. An incredible insight into the daily fight for survival happening behind closed doors Australia-wide. This book is not just for people wishing to find the strength to leave a violent relationship or heal emotional scars from past relationships. This book is for every mother, father, son, daughter, best friend or colleague of someone who has experienced violence.
Paul Ferry, Executive Director, Safe Haven Community

The individuals who penned their stories in this book, of what would have been an immensely painful chapter of their lives, are truly selfless. Through their words, they provide hope to those who need it most – those who may be unsure of how to start the

rebuilding journey. It opens the door to the truth that, after the darkness, your inner light will shine again.
Annette Westermann, 2017 Westpac Foundation Ambassador

A truly inspirational read – although impossible to get through one story without tears. These survivors are very courageous, and we thank them for sharing their stories with us.
The Community Underwriting Team

Writing my story has changed my life. It has taken the perpetual loop of anxiety-streamed flashbacks and ordered it with dignity, flow and finally release. 'It' – the abuse story – has lost its grip on my life story. A chapter, yes, but not the final one. Here's to the one person that may read my story and gather hope to break free from Domestic Terror. Here's to all the other survivors' stories, and to the ones who need hope. May our lives continue to shine on triumphantly.
Author of Terror to Triumph *Chapter 12: To the One Who Loved and Hurt Me*

Some say bravery is going to war, some say it's facing your fears... sometimes, it's just having the courage to choose to survive. These stories are stories of survival, of bravery, and have touched my heart and soul.
Tegan Philpott, Mornings Presenter, ABC Mackay

This is not just another book.

It is domestic terror victims' voices heard, survivors' stories of strength and success shared.

May each word you read allow the brave, resilient, brilliant you to emerge.

May each page you turn guide you to a new chapter in your life.

THANK YOU

Behind the printing press, the book cover, each page and every keyboard strike are hours of dedication, late nights, early mornings, cups of coffee and timeline slippages. On every page are words dripping with tears, fear, anger, anxiety, resentment, disbelief and grief. These words transform to bravery, resilience, strength, relief, release and excitement for the future ahead.

Thank you to the authors who bravely stepped forward, who made themselves vulnerable to release their pain through a willingness to help others rebuild their lives. You receive no financial gain or personal recognition. You know who you are. This book was fuelled by your courage and strength and Broken to Brilliant's drive to make a difference. Together, through each story, we share an easier way to rebuild life after domestic violence.

To everyone who supported the development of our second book *Terror to Triumph* we thank you for your time, effort, dedication, and belief that our book will make a positive impact on the lives of others.

For helping fund the book we thank:
- Community Underwriting for funding the writing workshop
- The Community Gambling Benefit Fund for funding the editing and publishing.

We thank the writing workshop presenters and supporters:
- Belinda Pollard, Small Blue Dog Publishing
- Fiona Ware, women's advocate, facilitator and children's author
- Rhonda Brown, Being Unbreakable
- Mercy Place and their supportive, caring staff
- Keifer Miller, Club Vitality
- Jane Rushton
- Sharon Wilks, WellWorkers.

Thank you to those who provided words of encouragement. You kept the fire burning.

Kate and Andrea

"It's not about how much we give but how much love we put into giving." Mother Teresa

FROM THE DIRECTORS OF BROKEN TO BRILLIANT

Founding the charity Broken to Brilliant and releasing stories of rebuilding life after domestic violence has been a desire since living through domestic violence. Rebuilding my life after domestic violence was not easy. Through the charity's work and with the dedicated directors, it is an honour to be able to help others to navigate their next chapter. We want survivors to feel worthy, valued, cared for, not alone and supported in their journey. To be their own brave, resilient and brilliant self. May each page you turn guide you to a new chapter in your life.

Kate

Founding Director, Broken to Brilliant

I am honoured to be one of the founding directors of the charity Broken to Brilliant. It means more to me than assisting a charity. It is hope, it is courage, it is education, support, caring and inspiration all wrapped together in love. Love for the brave survivors who stand up to make a difference, to help break the cycle of domestic violence and mentor fellow survivors to create a new chapter in their lives. Any change this charity can make could mean a world of difference in someone's future, and of this I am proud. I will continue to work for those changes.

Andrea

Founding Director, Broken to Brilliant

I am honoured to be a director for the charity Broken to Brilliant. Working with dedicated and truly driven founding directors who endlessly prove that survivors of domestic violence can rebuild their lives, is nothing but inspirational. Our tireless efforts to raise funds, apply for grants, hold workshops and publish the stories of survivors while building the charity's governance structure has been at times overwhelming, yet fulfilling. I believe that my contribution will provide Broken to Brilliant with a governance structure to grow and expand our incredible achievements.
Margaret
Director, Broken to Brilliant

If I could change just one life, one family from following down the dark, sad path marred by domestic violence, then my struggle has been worth it. Sharing that struggle through our own collective stories in *Terror to Triumph* strengthens our courage and determination to speak out and be heard.
Linda
Director, Broken to Brilliant

FOREWORD

I was young and brilliant when I met him. When I left, in my late 30s with children to protect, I was a terrified Broken Soul trying to put one foot in front of the other, trying to be a good role model for my children. I was trying to be Brilliant again.

At a domestic violence support group, I met one of the founders of the charity Broken to Brilliant. We had an instant connection, as we shared similar domestic violence experiences and were both health professionals. We became friends and supported each other in our journey of recovery, over a ten-year period and great distances. Together, yet thousands of kilometres apart, we have both undertaken advocacy work for victims of domestic violence.

I spend a lot of my time raising awareness about domestic violence and its impact, and how professionals can change their practice to help domestic violence victims. My first public speaking engagement was to over 700 people at the 20th Silent Domestic Violence Memorial March in Perth. I was again invited to speak at the 25th Silent March, where I spoke about my involvement in the book *Broken to Brilliant: Breaking Free to Be You After Domestic Violence, Stories of Strength and Success*.

The process of sharing my story made me realise that my words can change lives. My words can make people realise they are in unsafe and disrespectful relationships. My simple words from my humble heart CAN make a difference.

When a group of domestic violence survivors comes together as a collective to share their stories, our words and stories are even more powerful.

We can proudly say that the book *Broken to Brilliant* has been placed on refuge and shelter beds across Australia and overseas, providing hope and inspiration to domestic violence survivors. Our words and our stories are helping to change lives daily. It was heartwarming to hear one reader say:

> *'I read your book while in a refuge ... it inspired me to set up my online business, so I am now financially free.'*

Our stories of strength and success are making a difference. We are changing lives daily and helping others to be Brilliant.

Domestic violence should be renamed 'domestic terror'. Terrorism is a threat to commit an act with the intention to coerce, influence or intimidate. The act causes death, serious harm, endangers people and property, health and safety. Look at the response of the government, the media and the whole of society to terrorism! We need this scale of response to tackle the terrorists that are operating behind closed family doors, causing immeasurable harm to our women, our children and to some men. I felt like I was living in Domestic Terror.

This belief that we are facing terrorism from within was the inspiration for the name of the second book in the Broken to Brilliant series – *Terror to Triumph: Rebuilding Your Life After Domestic Violence, Stories of Strength and Success.*

I am so incredibly proud of all the authors that have contributed their words to *Terror to Triumph*. God bless you all. Your words are powerful, your words will be heard, your voices WILL be heard! YOU WILL MAKE A DIFFERENCE!

I met a woman whose marriage was unsafe and disrespectful. At that time, I was in the process of writing my chapter for the first book, *Broken to Brilliant*. Sharing my story gave me the courage to ask her, 'Can you watch a speech I've presented on family and domestic violence? I would really like your feedback.'

Secretly, I wanted her to hear and see what my message could evoke. I also wanted to see her reaction in real time. My simple words, my shameful story, my embarrassing past – could that make a profound change in someone's life?

We sat in silence as she watched the video. She heard my words and listened to the gasps from my colleagues and the positive feedback they gave me for sharing my story. Her hand silently reached for mine on the sofa. I held her hand tightly, and in my peripheral vision I could see the tears cascading down her beautiful face. She spoke. 'Oh my God! That is MY story!'

With every hair standing up on the back of my neck, my heart pounding, this was MY affirmation! I needed to keep being 'Brilliant' and sharing my story because my words DO make a difference! The power of sharing stories of how to rebuild life after domestic violence/domestic terror is why we have this second book and why there will be more books written.

Each chapter shares how that person has rebuilt their life. The writer describes the different coping strategies, tools, tips, and tricks they have used to pick up the pieces of their life, to dust themselves off and to move forward to a happy and healthy future.

By reading this book you will gain an understanding of how domestic violence impacts lives, but you will find the focus of these stories to be educational and nurturing. Helping people to grow and realise they have the right to be loved unconditionally. To be in safe and respectful relationships. Not only for themselves, but also for their children, their family, and their friends.

We never know the impact we have on people's lives – the people that we meet every day. Just a simple word, a simple glance, a simple inspiration of kindness that connects with their soul, can help someone to get out of that desperate situation.

Domestic violence/domestic terror survivors are fully functioning members of society and high-achieving individuals. Just look at Anne O'Neill, Rosie Batty, and all the authors of these two books! With your support, survivors know no boundaries anymore.

My hope is that copies of our books are placed on every refuge bed throughout Australia. I spent time in a refuge for protection. The information and leaflets I was given were all written by 'professionals'. They certainly have their place, but I felt such a failure and an embarrassment. How the hell did an intelligent health professional end up needing to stay in a refuge, for her own protection from the person she loved and had chosen to have children with?

I would have loved to have one of these books back then. I could have connected with at least one of the chapters. I would have realised that continuing to love unconditionally could have led to the death of me and my children. I could have learned strategies to move forward into a happy and healthy future.

I encourage you to purchase this book and support the charity Broken to Brilliant to help break the cycle of domestic terror so that everyone can be safe, and loved unconditionally. You may think that domestic terror does not affect you, but it does. If it affects one person and their children, then it ripples and seeps into the fabric of our community and it is woven into our lives. It could be an acquaintance, a colleague, a friend, a family member – even your 'bestest friend'. Domestic terror affects one in three women in Australia at some point in their lives – one in two if you are an Indigenous Australian, from the Middle East or aged between 15 and 25 years of age.

YOU can make a difference by purchasing these books to grow your understanding, or supporting the campaign to Give a Book to a refuge bed.

Thank you from one survivor who struggled to get her life back on track, and is working at being a brilliant, triumphant me.

Nicola

CONTENTS

PRAISE FOR *TERROR TO TRIUMPH* iii

THANK YOU vi

FROM THE DIRECTORS OF BROKEN TO BRILLIANT viii

FOREWORD x

INTRODUCTION 1

CHAPTER ONE
The Silence of Shame... 12

CHAPTER TWO
Surviving the Lies and the Way Back Home............................. 28

CHAPTER THREE
You Can Create a New Life... 44

CHAPTER FOUR
Nothing Changes if Nothing Changes 59

CHAPTER FIVE
I Believe in Me.. 78

CHAPTER SIX
Without Apology... 93

CHAPTER SEVEN
Threads Woven Through Relationships 108

CHAPTER EIGHT
Boundaries, Balance and Priorities.. 123

CHAPTER NINE
Don't Look Back 135

CHAPTER TEN
Two Small Hands 148

CHAPTER ELEVEN
Nightmares of My Childhood.. 163

CHAPTER TWELVE
To the One Who Loved and Hurt Me....................................... 177

GLOSSARY 192

ENDNOTES 195

CONTACT NUMBERS 199

ALSO IN THIS SERIES.. 203

INTRODUCTION

'Putting pen to paper released all that hurt and connection to my past and set me free.'

HOW SHOULD SURVIVORS FEEL, AFTER WE HAVE LEFT? I AM NOT sure, but we did not feel what others expected us to feel.

My friend came bustling up to me with a big smile, rushing towards me, arms open, ready for an embrace, as she said in an upbeat tone, 'Congratulations! You're out.' I did not feel that congratulations were in order. I felt like a failure. My marriage, relationship and life had failed. I didn't feel like celebrating. There was a mixture of loss, grief, shame, anger, resentment, regret, uncertainty, relief and excitement. How can one person feel so many mixed emotions at once? It was certainly a confusing time. People would say I should be happy, though happiness was not what I felt.

As the years progressed, their tune changed: 'You're a man-hater.' Their words could not be further from the truth. It is ongoing fear and lack of trust that makes survivors hesitant – scared to meet someone like that again. But where could we go for help? Who would understand?

As domestic violence survivors, we knew only too well that there was limited support for long-term recovery. That's why we founded the charity Broken to Brilliant. We do not work in the crisis or transition phases, but rather help people rebuild their lives, using personal experiences and stories to share the journey that lies ahead.

It is therapeutic for survivors to share their life story in a way that doesn't deny the trauma, but conveys the person's strengths and resilience. They describe their survival and the solutions they put in place to recover after adversity. Voicing personal experience and using creative expression as a self-help tool[1] can facilitate healing from the trauma of domestic violence.[2] Stories of survival, recovery and remaking of self, following domestic and family violence have been found to be empowering.

These are the very reasons for our series of books on rebuilding life after domestic violence. We are creating roadmaps for recovery. Approaching the story in this way helps to restore hope for both the victim and the readers.[3]

The impact of family and domestic violence

The impact of domestic and family violence does not stop once you leave the abusive relationship. The effects continue to impact the survivor's everyday lives, wellbeing and aspirations. Many will continue to experience violence, threats and attempts to control their lives from their former partner. Most will not be able to continue in the same workplace. Many will need support from family and friends for immediate accommodation. They often need to move suburbs and even states to rebuild their life. Their social activities and connections to the community decrease and they experience depression, anxiety and a range of other mental and physical health issues.[4] One study found that the physical and mental health of women who experienced domestic violence was 'consistently worse' after 16 years than those who had not experienced abuse, and these effects could last a lifetime.[5]

There has not been a lot of research into how survivors of domestic violence fully achieve psychological and physical wellbeing as they encounter the demands of creating a new life.[6,7] The Victorian Royal Commission into Family Violence 2016 found that the 'current responses to family violence do not sufficiently emphasise recovery and restoration and may even impede it. The ultimate objective of the family violence system must be that victims, including children, can recover and thrive at their own pace'.[8]

Domestic and family violence is emotional, social, financial, verbal, sexual and physical abuse, where one family member dominates another.

One partner in a relationship attempts, by physical or psychological means, to dominate and control the other. The relationship can be either heterosexual and homosexual, and the abuse of power can continue after separation. In the large majority of cases, the offender is male and the victim female.[9,10] The perpetrator controls their partner through fear, for example, by using violent or threatening behaviour.[11] It is a pattern of behaviour that escalates over time, slowly eroding the victim's confidence and ability to leave.[12]

Domestic violence includes:
- physical violence – slaps, shoves, hits, punches, pushes, being thrown down stairs or across the room, kicking,

- twisting of arms, choking, and being burnt or stabbed
- sexual assault or sexual violence – rape, sexual assault with implements, being forced to watch or engage in pornography, enforced prostitution, and being made to have sex with friends of the perpetrator
- psychological and emotional abuse – controlling behaviours such as control of finances, and isolation from family and friends.[13]

The World Health Organisation has found that 35% of women worldwide have experienced either intimate partner violence or non-partner sexual violence in their lifetime, and 38% of murders of women are committed by an intimate partner.[14]

The Australian Institute of Health and Welfare has assembled the following statistics about violence based on data from the Australian Bureau of Statistics (ABS) as a result of a current or previous partner. Men are more likely to experience violence from strangers and in a public place; women are most likely to know the perpetrator (often their current or a previous partner) and the violence usually takes place in their home. One in six Australian women and one in 16 men have been subjected to physical and/or sexual violence.

- Almost one in four (23%) women and one in six (16%) men have experienced emotional abuse.
- Almost one in five women (18%) and one in 20 men (4.7%) have experienced sexual violence (sexual assault and/or threats).
- Each day, on average, almost eight women and two men were hospitalised after being assaulted.

- Each week, one woman was killed as a result of violence.
- Each month, one man was killed as a result of violence.

People who as children witnessed partner violence against their parents were 2–4 times as likely to experience partner violence themselves (as adults) as people who had not. Nearly 2.1 million women and men witnessed violence towards their mother by a partner, and nearly 820,000 witnessed violence towards their father, before the age of 15.

Domestic violence is the leading cause of homelessness for women with children. In 2016–17, about 72,000 women, 34,000 children and 9,000 men seeking homelessness services reported that family and domestic violence caused or contributed to their homelessness.

Family violence occurs at higher rates for Indigenous Australians than for non-Indigenous Australians. Indigenous homicide victims were killed at twice the rate of non-Indigenous victims. Indigenous women were 32 times more likely to be hospitalised due to family violence than non-Indigenous women, while Indigenous men were 23 times more likely to be hospitalised than non-Indigenous men.[15]

The financial cost of violence against women and their children has been estimated at $22 billion.[16]

For children, exposure to domestic violence increases their risk of mental health, behavioural and learning difficulties in the short term, and of developing mental health problems later in life.[17] Women who have been exposed to violence have a greater risk of developing a range of health problems including stress, anxiety, depression, pain syndromes, phobias, somatic and medical symptoms. They report poorer physical health overall, are more likely to engage in practices that are harmful to their health and experience difficulties in accessing health services.[18] The long-term impacts of domestic violence include post-traumatic stress disorder, depression, eating disorders, early onset menopause and negative impacts on income, home-ownership and superannuation.[19] Emotions that stem from abuse – including distrust, bitterness, loneliness, anxiety, sadness, fear, shame, and confusion – can persist after leaving the abuser and affect the process of recovery.[20] There is less research about the long-term impacts of domestic violence on men. The studies that have been undertaken have shown that men are less likely to report the abuse, and suffer from poorer mental health such as depression.[21] For both male and female victims there is increased risk of poor health, depression, substance use, chronic disease, chronic mental illness, and injury.[22]

Violence has been woven into the accepted blanket of our lives and it is smothering our society. We need to unpick the fabric of society and cast new stitches of RESPECTFUL relationships, so we can ALL live and love and be free to choose life and laughter.

While we continue approaching domestic violence as a gendered issue we continue to create a divide. This divide deepens the division between men and

Respectful
Relationships
Emotionally
Supportive
Positive
Enriching
Caring
Togetherness
Friendship
Understanding
Love

BROKEN
to Brilliant

women. It perpetuates inequality and pits the genders against each other. As Jackson Katz said in his Ted Talk 'Violence Against Women is a Men's Issue': men and boys are also being abused by men.

What is needed is for men and women to work together to break the silence. This will create a radical change and transformation so that future generations won't have the level of tragedy that we are dealing with daily.

The impact of our series of books

In 2016, we were proud to launch our first book in this series, *Broken to Brilliant: Breaking Free to Be You After Domestic Violence, Stories of Strength and Success.* Hundreds of these books have been gifted to domestic violence survivors in shelters and refuges, or to other services that support domestic violence survivors as they rebuild their lives. These books have been donated by generous and caring people through our 'Give a Book' campaign and through grants.

We conducted an anonymous online survey and found that our other readers included domestic violence survivors or their friends, professionals who work with domestic violence victims, and also people who have no experience of domestic violence. All readers said they found the book inspiring and helpful. It educated them about domestic violence and strategies to rebuild lives. Most readers reported that they experienced personal growth after reading this self-help book.

We were encouraged by comments like these:
- 'Excellent insight to surviving domestic violence and good tips for hard times in general.'
- 'So much focus has been on helping women get out of the situation (which is needed) but this is the first book I have seen that helps you once you are out of the situation and getting back on your feet … This book gives me hope that I can do it.'
- 'Congratulations to the authors for sharing – very validating and practical information for domestic violence.'
- 'Gives hope to others experiencing domestic violence and the choices they can make to have a new beginning.'
- 'It's inspiring and has good, solid advice.'
- 'Thank you for pulling this amazing, timeless project together. Such a valuable resource for everyone involved in rebuilding lives after domestic violence.'

The book also had an impact on its authors. The ten *Broken to Brilliant* writers said they would recommend the writing process to other survivors. Most experienced personal growth through the writing process and felt that it was therapeutic.

Overall, the authors found that writing their story helped to turn a bad experience into a good one. They said it gave meaning to their experience, set them free and helped them to focus on the positives of what they have achieved. They felt the *Broken to Brilliant* book would become a keepsake, ensuring their experience was not forgotten, and that it would help their family members understand. Knowing their story was going to serve others in the same situation made the process humbling, added a sense of purpose and worth to their lives, and they felt honoured to be involved.

However, they also felt embarrassed, found it hard to turn their story into eloquent words, and feared negative responses from family and friends – or that their ex-husband may read it. A common statement among the authors was: 'My story is not good enough – I'm not brilliant enough to be in a book titled *Broken to Brilliant*.' This lack of worth stemmed from a sense of shame: 'I'm one of *those* women.' They worried that their story wasn't bad enough, that no-one would listen or believe them, or that if their solution was faith it would not be acceptable.

After sharing their story there was an overall 30% improvement in their belief that their story was worthy of being shared. They found the process of writing their stories to be cathartic. It allowed the authors to reflect on how far they had come.

The authors said:
- 'If I can make it through apathy and suicidal thoughts and come to this place now, it is possible for [the readers] too.'
- 'Amazingly, I no longer feel like that was my life. I am so far removed from it now.'
- 'Putting pen to paper released all that hurt and connection to my past and set me free.'
- 'It allowed me to take a step back and actually recognise the things I got through and what steps I actually took.

To see the beauty and the power of my strengths vs the weakness and brokenness. It showed me that there was value to my life and my story and that I can turn my pain into purpose to help serve others.'

Professionals who work in refuges and shelters have said that they have found the book very helpful, as women can relate to the stories and the stories are all different. They use the book as a sample to help other women with their story and to comfort them, supporting women towards resilience. Their clients have said:

- 'This sounds like my story.'
- 'Can I take the book with me when I leave?'
- 'This book gives me hope that I can get through this.'

Broken to Brilliant has been featured in newspapers, radio and television news. It received a bronze award in the self-help category of the eLit awards, a global program committed to illuminating and honouring the very best of English language digital publishing.

Terror to Triumph

When we saw the impact the book *Broken to Brilliant* has had on people's lives – how the words from the book breathed hope into people's hearts, how it gave them a spark that jump-started a new chapter in their lives, and how the power of people's stories created ripples of recovery and repair – we could not turn away and stop these ripples of healing.

And so the concept for *Terror to Triumph* emerged.

We wanted to enhance our support for the authors, so this

time we held a four-day live-in writing retreat. The program included art therapy, personal writing coaching, workshops on writing technique, a burning ceremony to release the past, and positive affirmation activities. Eleven women and one man attended. The authors said that the support we provided felt authentic as they felt loved, valued and heard. Trust was built among the group. The retreat changed their thinking. They felt more confident and encouraged. It opened their minds to alternative self-care methods. One person said, *'I leave a different person. There is no doubt about that.'*

Each author has been brave to step forward to share their story.

The result is twelve powerfully-written stories, describing the terror each one experienced and the additional challenges encountered from a system that is supposed to help and support. Most importantly, each story details the practical steps taken physically, emotionally, psychologically and spiritually to build new lives. The authors share how they went about their ongoing recovery and reclaimed self to reach a sense of triumph.

We salute each one for their courage and dedication, and hope this book will bring change and possibility into your life, too.

Andrea and Kate
Founding Directors, Broken to Brilliant

CHAPTER ONE

THE SILENCE OF SHAME

'I felt powerful and in control as I triumphantly walked by him.'

I HAD BEEN CHURNING ABOUT IT FOR WEEKS. *ASK HIM. DON'T BE SO GUTLESS!* All I wanted was to be able to take my children to visit my family.

Finally, I said the words. As they left my lips I watched his eyes glaze over. The switch had flipped, and I knew I was in for it. A feeling of dread washed over my trembling body. 'Run!' my reeling mind screeched in silence.

The intensity of his rage spurred my retreat. Yet I was too slow. He pinned me to the wall with a hand around my throat, clenched fist digging into the flesh of my cheek. Frothing at the mouth, spit flying everywhere, he yelled, 'Do you know how easy it would be for me to smash your face in?'

My brain dimmed. A foggy haze swirled around me as the air was sucked out of my lungs. He picked me up like a rag doll and threw me across the floor. The searing pain as I landed caused me to cry out.

I became aware of my children's presence. 'Dad! Dad! Please, please stop!'

Jarred by the distress on their faces and the gut-wrenching fear they might get injured, I whispered, 'I'm okay,' in an attempt to soothe them. They clung to me, trying to shield me. Despite their pleas, he came at me again.

A few weeks earlier, in an apparently futile attempt to stop the abuse, I had moved out of our bedroom. 'Take me back!' he demanded. 'Take me back.' I uttered not a word while cowering in the corner with my children clinging to me, sobbing. 'If you don't take me back then you can watch me shoot myself in the head.'

I gasped in horror – I knew who the bullets would hit first. The children's pleading intensified. 'Dad! Dad! No! No! No!' It did nothing to stop his rage. As he tried to drag me into the room where the gun was kept I grabbed onto the furniture, and held on with every ounce of strength my battle-weary body could summon. I knew without a doubt that to lose my grip would mean my children would lose their lives.

My thoughts didn't go to saving myself. I had accepted, long before, that I would die at his hands. I would give up every breath, every heartbeat I had left, before I would let him do that to my children.

This episode lasted for hours but he eventually gave up, leaving me lying limply on the floor, my traumatised children still clinging to me. My battered body so numb, that I felt like an empty shell. It was a struggle to even roll over in bed that night due to the pain.

Despite this battle to the very edge of life, I would not back away nor give in this time. The little spark of light still flickered ever so dimly, deep within me. On that dark night I swore silently to myself, 'No-one will ever do this to us again.'

***

Looking back on my relationship, there were a couple of 'aha moments' – which in hindsight would be better called 'uh-oh moments' – as I slowly came to grips with my stark reality. I had been conditioned to take so much, desensitised and disconnected from my thoughts, emotions, and body. I had become blind to the seriousness and the risks.

It slowly dawned on me that, despite my attempts to shield my children from the abuse, they were acutely aware of what was going on. I finally understood the role I was undertaking by complying with all his disturbed, twisted and controlling behaviours and that it could no longer continue. Living this life was robbing my children of all the happiness and love that they deserved, and their childhood was slipping by so quickly. The tipping point was looking into the eyes of my children and witnessing their torment and distress. The damage it was doing to them had become undeniable. I was the only person who could stop this. Unless I did, my children had no chance at all.

***

I was five years into the relationship before it dawned on me that this was domestic violence. My unsettled gut instinct and my brain finally connected. I can hear so many people say, 'Really? How blind can you be?' You would be surprised just how much of an expert these perpetrators are at hiding their true selves.

I remember the day the lights came on for me like it was yesterday. A police officer had been invited to my workplace to talk about the common signs of an abused woman. As he began, I glanced down at my cup of coffee sitting in my hands and noticed them trembling. Puzzled by my response I let my gaze drift around the room, watching intently the faces of those around me. Why was I the only one who seemed so unsettled?

As the officer described the behaviours of the abuser I grappled with an overwhelming sense of familiarity. He was describing my husband. The physical response from my body as I connected the dots hit like a sledgehammer. I gasped. A wave of nausea washed over me leaving the taste of vomit in my mouth. While I sat there, vividly aware of an internal struggle between my mind and body, one of the staff said, 'Why don't they just stand up to him? I would never put up with that rubbish.' An agreeing murmur echoed around the room.

The shame of hearing that shocked me. Blood drained from my face and my fragile, frozen heart shattered silently.

The shame silenced me. I built a wall to block others from seeing what was happening to me. The wall I built to shield me from the shame was also the biggest barrier to getting out. My fortress became my prison.

It haunts me today knowing just how helpless and alone I was. It was as if I mattered to no-one except my children. My love for my children and my beloved animals was the only thing that kept my spark alive. They were my only source of joy during those years with him. I can't recall any happy memories with him directly. There was never a period of remorse or honeymoon phase for us. He was a hard, cruel person who took joy in hurting others.

I had become his puppet and was dancing along to his tune. To the independent young woman I had been growing up, this was incomprehensible. For far too long my voice was silent. Not a single whisper escaped my lips. Fear was my constant companion and we knew each other very well.

It's interesting for me to look at the 'signs of domestic violence' through the lens of a mature woman, rather than the young teenager I was when I first met him. What began as minor ripples early in the relationship became a tsunami in the end. Of course, if a man treated me at the beginning how I was treated at the end, there's no way our relationship would have even lasted two weeks – but that's not the way it works.

The difficulty lies in recognising the hidden subtle flags early. They can often be misinterpreted in the toxic thrill of a new relationship. Signs for me looking back were his insistence on getting engaged and having a baby, and his concerns about things he had heard my family and friends saying about me behind my back.

The psychological and emotional abuse was there from the start. He would go over and over previous relationships until I burst into tears, then he would reassure me how much he loved me. On one hand, he would push me away, and then on the other he would suck me back in again. He knew just how far to push things at the start so that he didn't lose me.

His need to control all aspects of my life surfaced early as well, although he assured me it was for my own good. At that point, I believed him. The things I did, who I was friends with, where we lived, what I was allowed to do. There was no physical violence for the first few years, and when it began it started with slaps and pushing.

A couple of comments about things he had done in his

previous relationships sent chills down my spine. He was very closed about what had happened, but bragged about the look of fear on their faces. I know I should have asked questions and dug deeper. Not to him, as I know he would have just lied to me, but to his family and those around him.

What saddens me is that I wasn't the first and wasn't the last woman he abused. I live in hope that my children were his only children, and no others had to grow up with so much heartache. The damage that is done to the children, especially at a young age, is far-reaching and so hard to heal.

He would often tell me that all the things he did to me were to make me a stronger person. In the end, it backfired on him. He had made me so strong that no matter what he threw at me I would not give in.

***

I remember many years ago hearing someone at work joke about how cold I was. 'Ice Queen,' they laughed behind my back. Those taunting words were like an icy hand gripping my heart, squeezing the life out of it. As their words echoed in my mind, a haunting memory flooded my senses: flung onto the bed, a pillow held over my face, suffocating me because I had refused to answer him after hours of interrogation about why I was late home from work. I just lay there and waited for it to end. 'In many ways you are right,' my inner voice threw back at those workmates. 'How else could I go on with life as if nothing had happened?'

Years later, after I was free from him, people came forward and told me things they had noticed such as red marks on my throat. Yet they never spoke up or reached out. It is so heart-wrenching that people can turn a blind eye. I guess they just preferred not to get involved. It was easier that way for them.

Little by little I gradually began to thaw, sparked by the very fire that he could never extinguish. Tragically, it took another ten years from the first realisation that I was being abused to when I finally started the battle to get out. Something within me shifted and the strength and courage that had kept me alive came to the forefront.

In order to save my children, I knew I had to reach out and tell someone. At first, I used anonymous assistance phone lines. I made sure I called from a phone he wouldn't be able to trace. It gave me the confidence and courage to start planning how to get out of this mess as safely as I could.

I finally reached out to trusted friends. The look on their faces as I told them some of the things he did to me I will never forget. One of the most difficult things for me was to actually speak the words out loud and see someone's reaction. It was profoundly terrifying yet at the same time so reassuring that I had been heard. As each word escaped my lips the certainty grew that I was following the right path. From this point forward, I knew there was no going back.

I walked away from that life with a hard shell around me and it's taken a long time for that to soften. I was very hard on myself and would often tell people that it was my choice to stay in the relationship, therefore I was responsible for what happened to me. I guess that approach got me through a very painful time in my life. My survival patterns have been hard to shake but now I live life with no regrets and a lot more self-compassion.

Too much time is wasted on regrets. I cannot change the past and I will not let my past rob me of a happy, peaceful future. I have turned all the heartache, pain and sadness into determination, strength, and wisdom. I hold no hatred or anger towards him. They are emotions that steal from you the very essence of life.

Dissociation – disconnecting from thoughts and feelings, the well-developed skill that made me an 'ice queen' – was robbing me of a rich and full life. How could I turn from walking through life as if in a fog to a life full of brightness, connection, and aliveness? That is where my discovery of new possibilities began. I found a helping profession where I could turn my dissociation into an appropriate tool. I now use my own experiences to support others, and consciously switch on and off when needed.

***

My incredible, courageous children helped me rebuild my life. I have watched them over the years blossom into compassionate, warm and wise young adults. They were able to get me to face the wrongness of what he was doing to us. They were able to speak out in their own voices to others around us when we got out. I was surprised by the power of their words and how much they had been aware of, despite my attempts to hide it. It was our shared, lived story and it was very powerful for us to speak out together. Our story has united us and the strength of that has supported us through the difficult times.

A couple of my work colleagues, now lifelong dear friends, stood by my side through some pretty frightening times. Their emotional and physical support helped keep me on the path to freedom. It was almost impossible for me to ask for help but they knew instinctively what was needed. It still brings tears to my eyes how these beautiful people literally saved our lives.

Lifelong learning also has been vital to rebuilding my life. Spending time and money on my own education before I left, as well as after, has created so many opportunities for me. During the years of abuse, my escape was burying my head in a book. I had always loved reading and was fascinated by how many interesting things you could learn. There is power in learning and studying. I believe it is through learning and growth we truly heal. The personal satisfaction and sense of achievement associated with this have been life-changing for me as well. It has given me the ability to secure good employment and regain financial control in my life. My passion for people and animals has also blossomed through my studies and it is through learning about how to help them that I have inadvertently helped myself and my family.

Pretty much all the relationships I had in my life were completely focused on meeting the needs of others, so I have had to do a lot of work connecting with my own needs. Even today, I still struggle with what my wants, desires, and needs are. I walked away from my marriage with literally no idea. With the support of psychotherapy, I have much more awareness of my patterns, behaviours and how I respond to certain situations. The increase in awareness gives me a more conscious choice. I have always been very aware of my triggers as they spoke loud and clear. I wanted to connect with the other parts of me that had long been forgotten. I struggled to let go of unhealthy patterns I had formed as part of my survival that were holding me back from peace and happiness. One that stood out was isolation – it was as if I had forgotten how to make meaningful connections with others and myself.

Now I have created space within my world, allowing me to connect more fully with those around me. My body's response is the most honest and trustworthy guide to understanding whether something sits well with me or not. I can still be hijacked by emotions and thoughts which can go from a 1 out of 10 to 10 out of 10 in a split second. 'Catastrophiser' thought patterns cause my imagination to run wild, resulting in a cascade of anxiety until my body is trembling with fear. Now as soon as I'm aware the catastrophiser thought pattern is emerging, I recreate the scene in a way that soothes me.

I have taken great delight in creating my own safe space in my home, where I consciously sit, pause and check in with how I am travelling. I had become such an expert in filling up every last second of my day (busyness) as a way of escaping my past. I found it hard to stay in one spot for long, but now I have created a space just for me to sit, breathe and ground myself.

My deep connection with horses has been another support. People often ask me when my love of horses began. My reply is always, 'Before I was born.' I have drawn on their power, strength, and wisdom all my life. They are incredible, spirited and sensitive creatures who are so honest and open. Having them in my life has been one of my greatest gifts. Even during the darkest times of my life, I was able to wrap my hands around their neck, bury my head in their mane and cry my river of tears.

Galloping along the ridge, the wind in my face, the thunder of hooves beneath me, I would feel the freedom that I longed for. Even if it was only for a moment, it gave me the hope that I would be free again. Having them in my life allowed me to love and be loved in a way where I felt nurtured and protected in a world where there was little of that.

An immense change I have undergone is being able to find the other side to my fierce warrior woman. I still adore her and know she will always be at my side. I knew in my heart in order to find peace, I needed to find that other softer side. That harsh part of her which had served me very well was also holding me back. She is a key part of my survival mode, so there initially was a great deal of resistance in letting her go. She hasn't gone very far and still pops up from time to time when I need her. The difference is, she now comes when I call her, and I welcome her with compassion and care.

In opening up my softness I allow my vulnerabilities to surface. In the past I saw them as weakness because they were often used as weapons against me, to torture, manipulate and control me. Now I welcome, embrace and truly recognise them as my strengths and supports. Developing awareness has given me clarity, courage, and confidence to see who I have become, while not forgetting the path I followed to get here.

I spent almost all of my adult life living in fear. Even after I ended that relationship, my whole being had been conditioned to fear and I simply couldn't switch it off. One way I have been able to overcome the power fear had over me was to track how my body responds to situations. I check in with my body to notice telltale signs like trembling or churning. If I notice any I ground myself by taking a breath, feeling the air in my lungs and the connection of my feet to the earth.

As funny as this may sound, I started to reprogram my brain, almost like tricking it. I would say to myself out loud, as I noticed the wave of fear creeping over my body, that I am safe now. I am safe now. Louder and louder, over and over. My heart rate would drop, the trembling would settle and I would hear the power of my voice. The more I practised, the quicker and easier it was to settle. At first, it felt awkward and clunky, but I persisted till my sense of safety became tangible. Little by little, it became so comfortable and natural. Now I can say the words in my mind and know in my heart I am safe and have found a place of peace.

I have done a lot of work around understanding my triggers. Not only of understanding what they are but also of looking at them in more depth. I look back on all the abuse that was done to me, knowing at the time that there was very little outward reaction. It's inevitable that when you start to open up, both negative and positive emotions arise. I knew in my heart I would have to revisit this 'unfinished business'. How to do this without having a meltdown was probably the thing I feared most. I avoided it for years until slowly I found my way as I gradually developed and strengthened my supports. My past terrors were like my Medusa, the monster of Greek mythology with snakes for hair. Those who looked directly at her face turned to stone, but the hero managed to slay her by looking only at her reflection. I was petrified that I would completely shatter if I looked my past terrors in the eye. My supports were the reflective shield that allowed me to bring my Medusa into the light and destroy her.

My children have grown up into adults who had also been so traumatised by their past. In the early days after I left my husband, they had gone to counselling and things settled as we rebuilt our lives. Now they are young adults, I can see that they still carry many of the scars I do. Through my studies, I also have a much greater understanding of the impact of growing up in that environment – often minimised by people who haven't been exposed to such events. I realise now just how much damage staying in the relationship did to them. Being able to support them, watch them blossom and develop into young caring adults is healing for all of us. Without having done the earlier work on myself there is no way I could have had the capacity or skills to support them as I do now.

***

I had always dreaded the day I would cross paths with him again. I have continued to be triggered by flashes of what he did to the children, our pets and myself. I feared how my body, mind, and spirit would react if I ever saw him again. Fate would have it that many years later our paths did cross. I could hear the crunch of the gravel under my feet. Looking up, scanning the crowd, my gaze shifted to a figure. It was a figure I knew well. His gaze fixed on me. I felt my survival mode stir ever so slightly as calmness wafted over me. *Look at me now. Look at who I have become despite what you did.* My response astounded me and reinforced just how much I have healed and grown. I was no longer the vulnerable, scared woman, alone with my children, under his control. I was now a confident, educated woman who had found her voice.

I felt powerful and in control as I triumphantly walked by him.

Finally, after so many years, I am making my almost-forgotten passions come back to life. It always broke my heart to have to let go of my dreams and wipe them from my memory. I have made them come alive again. I am free to make my own choices and to watch my children grow up without fear. Free to reconnect with my family and friends. To heal enough to consider the possibility of an intimate relationship with someone who doesn't try to dominate, control or hurt me. To trust another person in this way is something I never thought would be possible. Free to laugh, love, smile and speak out without fear of the consequences. I am out of his shadow with a successful career, beautiful home, wonderful family, friends and of course my precious herd of horses. My life has blossomed.

LIGHTS

CHECKLIST
☑ ____
☑ ____
☐ ____

TERROR to Triumph

There were many things that helped me rebuild my life. Follow this path, which LIGHTS the way for you to find your inner self, to be free, to laugh, to smile and to speak out without fear. Make your own choices, bring your power to life, and live a life of your dreams.

LIFELONG LEARNING: Spending time and money on my own education has created so many opportunities for me. There is power in learning and studying. It opens up so many possibilities. The key to healing is through learning and growth.

INNER SELF: Creating space within myself and my world allowed me to connect more fully with those around me. I now find my body's inner response is the most honest and trustworthy guide to understanding whether something is my truth. My body is the best gauge of how I'm travelling. I have created my own safe space in my home, which allows me to sit, breathe, and ground my inner self. Through my work on my inner self I have also been able to connect with my inner softness and let that out. I 'check in' with my body and can calm my inner self by saying out loud: 'I am safe now. I am safe now.'

GET THERAPY: Seek support from a psychologist, therapist or counsellor to help you become aware of your patterns, behaviours and how you respond to certain situations. They can help you work through unhealthy patterns.

Horses: Having horses in my life allowed me to love and be loved in a way where I felt nurtured and protected. I have drawn on their power, strength, and wisdom so many times.

Triggers: Learn to understand what your triggers are and look at them in more depth. Revisit your unfinished business.

Support: Find ways to support yourself. I found that support from those with 'lived experience' is often the most effective. Horses or other animals can provide their own kind of support.

CHAPTER TWO

SURVIVING THE LIES AND THE WAY BACK HOME

'Day by day, step by baby step, each day a new strategy, I was filling with anticipation and excitement, because there was something to wake up for. I was surfacing.'

I WAS USED TO THE DIFFICULT TIMES AND DIFFICULT FEELINGS, yet nothing would prepare me for, or explain the terror I would feel, when he started coming home at two in the morning. He would crawl into bed and turn his back to me, wordless. Not one word. Every night. Like any girl, I cajoled, I pleaded, asked politely, was sweet, was angry. No communication from him. Stony silence.

It became too much, this crazy way of connecting. Soon my young-girl's dreams began to shatter. Dreams of love, of meaning, of being held, being cared about, of having meaningful conversations way into the night, of building a family made from love and helping the world become a better place.

Not only did my dream shatter, I began to splinter. Walking by a quaint little jewellery shop one day, I caught sight of a little crystal pram next to a little crystal palace. Subconsciously, I knew that this was what my heart and soul wanted. The reality was that I was living in a dark, dangerous fairytale. Instead of the archetypal prince of love, I'd found his evil twin.

After threatening to leave him one too many times, he finally offered a few words by way of explanation. 'I'm out playing cards with friends. Stop being so paranoid.' But I knew all was not as it seemed. And here came the first big lesson: trust your gut. We were newly married. What friends are that important to be with every night till two in the morning? Was he a gambler? Was he commitment-phobic? The truth turned out to be more painful.

No amount of warm milk, baths before bed, chats with friends or light reading could calm me down. The terror was building with each consecutive night. All alone, scary thoughts, no relief. Something was terribly wrong. The gaslighting had begun.

***

Gaslighting[*] is both a colloquial and a psychological word. The truth is twisted, turned in, blended to suit the lie of the teller. Soon, the receiver cannot tell what is the truth and what is a lie. Some gaslighters run very deep lies. Their external appearance is the only truth they show. Below that is a hidden iceberg of lies. Gaslighters play with the truth for dangerous outcomes and reasons.

Finding open letters and address books was not uncommon in our flat. He wrote in letters to friends overseas that he had two girlfriends. When confronted, he'd smirk and say, 'You've read it all wrong.' In the address books were many women's names

---

[*] Gaslighting is a type of manipulation designed to make the victim question their memories, perception, or sanity. The term comes from a stage play of the 1930s.

– all with disconnected or false numbers. I know – I tried calling them. There were no male names in the address books.

One day, a woman did answer these detective calls of mine. I was terrified. It turned out she was 18 years old and he been trying to woo her for a long time. Flowers, chocolates, cards, visits to her work where she was the receptionist. She had a boyfriend.

'I don't know what he wants,' she said. 'I've asked him many times to just leave me alone. I'm thinking of speaking to the police. I had no idea he was married. He's just sick!'

We made a plan. He tended to visit her while on his 'I'm going out to buy cigarettes' runs that lasted three hours.

***

The girl and I stage a sting.

He comes home with his pack of cigarettes.

Me: 'You said you were only going out for cigarettes.'

Him: 'That's right. Something wrong with your hearing?'

Me: 'Just wondering, because you always go out for a packet nearly every day then turn up three hours later. The shop is only on the corner, you know.'

He completely ignores me, walks through to the TV, turns it on, loud, and gets lost in the noise.

My phone rings. It's the girl. 'He's just been to my work,' she says. 'Where is he?'

'He's here,' I whisper.

'Great!' She hangs up, and rings him, while I am with him. I hear her. She is loud, and angry. She yells at him that she and I have met and the game is over.

He races to the balcony to finish the call. 'It's work,' he tells me. I follow him. He's starting to get very, very uncomfortable. 'It's work,' he says. 'Go back inside.'

'No, it's not!' I say.

'No, it's not!' yells the girl on the other end of the line.

He darts a look from the phone to me to the phone. She yells at him that if he does not leave her alone and stop this lie, she is going to the police for a restraining order. I hear her very, very clearly. He puts his hand over the mouthpiece and says to me, 'Crazy, crazy woman. Chasing me. Wants me.' And does the sign for crazy with a finger circling his ear.

Exhausted, I go back inside and go to bed.

***

There were other women everywhere we went. He had to touch, flirt, converse with them as I sat so lonely, forsaken in the corner. Women flirted openly with him in front of me.

All respect had left my life. I was alone with a sociopath. His friends slowly began to come to me with stories, unable to bear the guilt of holding the secrets.

'He's seeing other women. Lots of them,' one said.

'I saw him last Saturday, at the disco, with a blonde lady,' said another.

Friends would tell me he had tried to flirt and kiss them. I would confront him, and he would say that these people were 'jealous' and 'trying to break us up'. That I was being 'too sensitive', 'untrusting of him' and 'paranoid' and that it was 'unattractive'.

I said we seemed so unsuited – we hardly ever conversed, held hands or enjoyed our time together.

He said, 'Give it time. All I want is to be married and have children with you. We'll be married with kids in a big old church before you know it.' We had married in a small, strange civil ceremony. For a long time he had dangled 'The Promise' of a second ceremony, a big white church wedding with all our friends and family.

I dwindled from an energetic, happy, vibrant girl who would go out dancing two or three nights a week, so happy to be alive, to a phantom – always afraid, always hyper alert, not able to sleep. Soon, I was afraid to leave the flat.

Sleeplessness, racing thoughts, erratic breathing, and hours and hours of mindlessness in front of the TV became my new 'normal'. I withdrew from life. Gone were my friends, all supports, my interests and pastimes. Gone was my sleep, my confidence, my faith, my jobs. My beautiful life. All gone.

I became his puppet. He pulled the strings and I moved to his sickness. I tried to leave once, but having lost everything, I had no energy to fight. I felt hopeless and trapped. Without help, guidance or real care to break free from his web, I went back to him, defeated. He smirked at my return and held the door open wide for me to enter back into the mire.

***

Looking back, there were lots of red flags, but I had no experience of this kind of deliberately wicked behaviour, so I kept making the red flags turn normal. I desperately needed normal. My world was becoming anything but normal. And I had to hang on to at least the idea of normality if nothing else.

Bad idea, wrong strategy. Better idea, better strategy: listen to the warning signs. They are there for a reason – to keep you safe.

'To keep you safe.' How special is that? That we have these early warning signs, so that we can notice them – so we can leave, or stay away, or KEEP OURSELVES SAFE. That's normal behaviour, right? Healthy behaviour. But some of us have been so badly damaged by life, that our normal healthy instinct to protect ourselves is just not working as well as it should be.

His long, unexplained absences. His words and actions not adding up, the lack of loving emotions, the lack of interaction and conversations. The lack of affection and any interest in who I was. Scoffing at the things I held dear, like painting, drawing and reading. 'Not again!' he would say and roll his eyes, when I'd cry from the sheer exhaustion of the mind games and lies.

The controlling. The shaming. Once, on a rare night out, I wore a knee-length white skirt with a flowing sky-blue top. *Pretty smart*, I thought. Big hoop earrings, hair curled and flying over my shoulders. Made up, curled and hot. That's how I felt.

Instead, we left the party early. He didn't like the attention I was getting from other men. Once home, he turned to me and spat, 'This is why I don't go out with you. You never dress like a woman. Where is your cleavage? Your skirt is too long. Why are you wearing those earrings? You're an embarrassment!'

This guy was distorting my truth, and my reality. Everything that was right and meaningful to me, he was ridiculing and making wrong. On top of that, he piled so many layers of lies, untruths and deliberate distortion of his whereabouts that he damaged me psychologically.

Of course, I should have paid attention to all the early warning signs and red flags. If I had, I would have been free to continue a happy life. But it wasn't to be. Devious deceitful people were not in my orbit of friends. My friends were decent, good people. I had no armoury within me to fight this man because I'd never met anyone like this before.

So, I stayed for three years, until he got the Australian residency he had applied for through our civil marriage ceremony, and then he threw me out.

***

By then, I was very, very damaged. I still have post-traumatic stress from way back then. The lack of sleep, betrayal, abandonment, lies, deceit, ridicule, distress, loneliness I went through damaged me badly. Grief ate me up daily. I cried all the time: on the bus, on the train, in the street, at the shops. I could not stop crying. So, I stopped going outside.

I stayed indoors all the time. I slept a lot. I slept through two whole days once. Once he got his Australian residency, he told me, 'We have to separate because you fight with me too much.'

Kind relatives offered me a place to stay. I had withdrawn from all my friends, work interests, outdoor life. I stayed indoors, in bed, bundled with my damaged and disrupted self. Somehow, hoping that enough blankets and heat would return me to me.

It didn't work, and I fell further through the cracks. I left that home, unable to be still or normal or social. I needed me. But I had no job, no money, no friends, no support.

Many more bad things happened to me. I had no money other than some benefits that barely paid for my rent. Brave, alone, I tried to recover. Chronic fatigue set in. I didn't have enough money for clothes, food, power. Rent was late, food was scarce. I wore the same set of clothes for a long time. I gave up on living or even liking life. I didn't bother with grooming or my appearance. I still couldn't sleep. Fitful and waking up suddenly, jerking wide awake. I developed big grey circles under my eyes.

Aside from my dear mum and a couple of friends visiting, no-one was any real help, during the time I with him, or after. I was descending into a living hell. My kitchen had rats because it was the only part of town I could afford to rent. I could not change the nightmare that had enveloped me on every level – physically, mentally, socially, financially, spiritually.

***

I thought of taking my life. I almost did, but divine intervention saved me – and not for the first or only time. The 'other side' has always sent in the cavalry at the most pivotal moments.

On this particular night, listening to the scuffle of rats in my kitchen, I was on my knees in the dark room, among silhouettes of sparse furniture that I had managed to salvage from the streets. I was yet again, tearfully, trying to talk myself into possible scenarios for ending my life.

Suddenly, I felt a presence in the room. I heard something. It was like someone spoke to me. Someone very kind with great authority said to me, 'Yes, it is sad. Awful, tragic that no-one is here – unforgivable really.' It paused. 'But *you're* here,' it soothed, talking as if I mattered.

I mattered. I mattered to that being. Maybe it was my guardian angel. I don't know, but it worked. My guardian angel gave me the strength to fight, and, I did! I felt protected for the first time in a long time. It was all I needed. The battle was on to get well and come back.

***

I started by taking stock. Logical, rational stock. I had two degrees. I was an 'A' grade student – how on earth did I end up in such a mess? My beloved father had passed away. I was drowning in poverty, agoraphobia, chronic fatigue. No friends, no work, no sleep, no social life and I had developed chronic asthma that often progressed from not being able to breathe to almost passing out. It was a scary, scary time.

Going to counsellors and doctors did not help me. Our health system is just not equipped to work with survivors of abuse past the crisis stage. We have shelters and domestic abuse crisis services, but absolutely nothing for survivors past one year out. We are still hurting, suffering and spasming in the afterlife of abuse. Support and real help seemed not to be there – other than offers of antidepressants or expensive psychologist appointments that did not help, mentor, guide or coach me in my unique situation. Half-hearted or vague interest by health professionals.

My world had been hit by a nuclear bomb and no matter how much I spoke all I seemed to be getting was vague acknowledgment and pills. I needed more.

Because that voice had been there, because it had loved me for a moment, things started to change. I became rational. **I listed all my issues**: grief, lack of sleep, lack of money, lack of friends and self-esteem, agoraphobia, chronic fatigue, and asthma. Lack of motivation to work along with the lack of money.

I listed them all, and I started attacking each issue head-on. With little baby steps, but I started. I was weak and tired, a lot. I was hungry. I was done. But I kept going. Day by day, step by baby step, each day a new strategy.

Going to sleep was important now because there was something to wake up for.

I was filling with anticipation and excitement.

***

I started with a five-minute visit to the local park. I came back home. I did it! I had broken the agoraphobia grip. I never pushed myself and did only what I could do, and I rested a lot. But I did things. I fought against the hopelessness and inertia that owned me. I knew if I was to come back, if I was to recover, I had to fight hard against these two things.

Self-care became vital. It was the road back. I made better choices. For example, with the little money I had for food, I bought cheap but nutritional food, like vegetables, milk, packets of home-brand brown rice, home-brand cheese, fruit, and yoghurt. I had a healthier weekly menu. I bought at the thrift shops and discount stores – affordable, nice clothes and shoes. My self-esteem shot up.

Feeling and looking better was instrumental. **Clean** hair, teeth, clothes and a clean home help in recovery. I started to look and feel 'normal'. I was starting to win over the agoraphobia.

Day by day, I gave myself **goals**:
- Walk up the street, then come back home. Only what I could do, but keep pushing through.

- Look around – why weren't others in such a bad place? They had money, jobs, possessions. **Money and finances** became important. I needed strategies to get back to work, back to the community. So, I worked out how much I could handle and respected myself and did that. At first, it was only three hours a week. As soon as I felt comfortable with being outside and around others, on transport, I went up to five hours, then casual work, then part-time and finally full-time. What a proud day that was! Fortunately or unfortunately, finances are a real thing, and we need to plan for money. It can make all the difference between a restful or anxious life.
- **Routines** became important. Going to sleep and waking up at the same time every day. Giving myself a cup of coffee and a piece of toast every morning.
- I started to follow goals based on the old wives' tales: **good sleep, rest, joy, friendship, exercise, community, time in nature, good food**. All precious advice and very therapeutic. I made sure I took a walk at least once a week somewhere beautiful in nature – the sea, a park, the country. I made time once a week to reconnect with an old friend. I made time for rest and quiet.

Through respecting my needs and self-care, I learned it mattered how I felt and looked and my self-esteem healed.

Through logic and rational thinking, I learned to put unhelpful emotions to the side and act proactively for myself. I acted **as if** I wasn't broken. I started acting and living **as if** I was already well. And I became well.

Through **self-respect** and **baby steps**, I conquered my asthma, agoraphobia and chronic fatigue. I took small, logical actions – for example, a few minutes, seconds, whatever I could handle each day outside my front door, as far as I could travel then back home. So I learned that it was okay, it was safe to be outside.

The psychological shift happened. And then I could carry on the work of being an adult in this society of ours. Managing my life: working, shopping, socialising, exercising and so on.

Connection with good people was also vital for recovery. No-one heals alone. I found kindness and belonging through the years with these people and I wish to thank them:

- the Brahma Kumaris for their peaceful, wise, gentle meditations
- the peace group I joined – all the wonderful conversations about ethical behaviour
- the evangelical church I was taken to. Thank you for the fellowship and care. I was there for a while after my separation
- the many friends I met along the way who cared about me and nurtured me
- the dear old friends who came back into my life
- my wonderful family who worked to help me through the aftermath
- the many wonderful jobs I have had, and the decent, good people I've gotten to work with.

Much love and thanks to all of them.

***

Where am I now? I was 30 when I left him. I'm in my mid-fifties now. It's taken a solid 20+ years to fully recover. I had to work at this day and night, rest, feel the pain and **never give up** when things failed and went pear-shaped (and they will).

I talked myself around, instead of catastrophising. I used nicer, safer words to myself in my head. I gave myself better, nicer scenarios and things I could do to not feel helpless. And then I would have a good night's sleep, and take the steps needed to address the latest challenge in the morning.

Things started to heal. The world, my world, became safer. I now speak up for myself and my boundaries. I keep myself safe and treat myself with the best self-care. I meet my own needs and have a life plan that has logical goals strategies and actions. If I 'fall' with an unhealthy choice, it doesn't matter, because I have my routines, friendships, family, groups, and self-care taking place now.

Since I broke free of that disturbing man and relationship, I have repaired my broken self-esteem and returned to work. I own a car, have saved money and earned a diploma. I have reconnected with my dear family and friends, made beautiful new friends by reconnecting with my passions, healed the asthma, chronic fatigue and agoraphobia that plagued me while I was with him. I have embraced and loved myself back to life.

There is no greater power or purpose than that of love. Life is good! I'm back to my passions and hobbies. I've always wanted to be a writer. The wonderful directors of the charity Broken to Brilliant asked me to write about my story. I hope it helps you find some relief. May God guide your journey, and may you always travel safe in this life.

Your inner self SURFACING

Start. Each day, day by day, just take step by baby step – each day a new strategy. This will help to keep you safe. Treat yourself with the best self-care and meet your own needs. Create a life plan, with logical goals, strategies and actions. Never give up. Take the time and your real inner self will begin **SURFACING**.

SELF-CARE AND SELF-RESPECT: Feeling and looking better was instrumental for me. Clean hair, teeth, clothes and a clean home help in recovery. Make better choices. For example, buy cheap but nutritional food, like vegetables, milk, packets of home-brand brown rice, home-brand cheese, fruit, and yoghurt. Create a healthier weekly menu. Buy clothes and shoes at thrift shops and discount stores. Your self-esteem will shoot up. Through respecting my needs and self-care, I learned it mattered how I felt and looked and my self-esteem healed.

U: You are worthy and valuable, you are inherently worthy for the sheer fact that you exist. Believe it.

RED FLAGS: Are relationship signs that can alert you to a dangerous future relationship. The warning signs can include that they have a sense of entitlement and don't talk through issues, everything is about them, they are overly critical about their previous partners, they constantly criticise and dismiss you, your lack of trust and communication. Listen to the warning signs. They are there for a reason: to keep you safe.

ROUTINES: Predictable, repetitive routines can be calming and help reduce anxiety, and exercise routines are beneficial as well. Go to sleep and wake up at the same time every day. Incorporate daily exercise such as walking.

FINANCES: Money and finances are important. You need strategies to get back to work, back to the community. Work out how much you can do, how much time you can work, and build up to working longer. Be proud of each step. Fortunately, or unfortunately, finances are a real thing, and we need to plan for money. It can make all the difference between a restful or anxious life.

ACTION: Use logical actions – for example, the strategy for conquering your issues. Take just a few minutes or seconds – whatever you can handle each day – so long as you take action.

CONNECTION: Connection to good people is also vital for recovery. No-one heals alone. Find kindness and belonging through different groups, such as yoga, meditation, churches, friends, family, work colleagues or other gentle, ethical, kind and respectful people.

IDENTIFY YOUR ISSUES: List all your issues such as grief, lack of sleep, lack of money, lack of friends and self-esteem, any health conditions, lack of motivation to work and others. List them all. Start attacking each issue head-on, with little baby steps. Keep going, day by day, step by baby step, each day a new strategy.

Never give up on yourself: Keep going and take baby steps, day by day. Work at this day and night. Rest, feel the pain and never give up when things fail and go pear-shaped (and they will).

Goals: Set yourself small goals, such as a good night's sleep, rest, joy, friendship, exercise, community, time in nature, good food. Take a walk at least once a week somewhere beautiful in nature – the sea, a park, the country. Make time once a week to reconnect with an old friend. Make time for rest and quiet.

© Broken to Brilliant

CHAPTER THREE

YOU CAN CREATE A NEW LIFE

'After leaving, I watch my children happily playing. It gives me strength, knowing that what I'm doing is right for all of us.'

MY STORY BEGINS WAY BEFORE THE DOMESTIC VIOLENCE EVER began and remember, this is written with hindsight. I was raised by a mother with mental health issues and a father with his head up his a__. Don't get me wrong, Dad had great intentions, but his strategy for coping was avoidance, and it still is.

At 16, I'm a cute, feisty little blonde with a wicked sense of humour and a mind of my own. I'm guessing my mother isn't coping so well with me, because she packs my belongings and deposits me at a caravan park. Dad doesn't notice me missing for two weeks.

Upon reflection, I don't think I was the most well-behaved teenager. Maybe better parenting might have changed my trajectory, but we can't change the past, only the future. All I can say is: lucky I had a job and was able to support myself.

I'm craving affection. I certainly don't get it at home and so the first guy who comes along, I fall instantly in love with.

This guy is hot, I mean *sizzling*. We end up moving in together after a whirlwind romance of four days, making-cosy in a

22-foot caravan made for two. Life is tough, but I'm in love and I get married. Do you like the way I said 'I', and not 'we'? Six years later, two kids later, a slightly larger 32-foot caravan and several affairs later, the 'I' ends.

I'm not in a good way. The man I'm supposed to spend the rest of my life with, the father of my children, obviously doesn't love me so I leave. I need help, there isn't any. I'm without income, two kids and two stripey bags containing a few saucepans, clothes and not much else.

Enter the dragon: six-foot, black hair, great tan and he just appears out of nowhere to rescue me and the kids.

We know each other through mutual friends and he's heard I'm in trouble. 'Stay with me, all you need to do is cook and clean and there's plenty of room. I work night shift, so you will have the place to yourself.' Given my circumstances and the too-good-to-be-true offer, I accept.

If only I'd known how these men target women in need. We now all know this as love bombing.*

This bloke has done his reconnaissance work and views me as a meal ticket. I know you may find this hard to believe, but he doesn't want to work, and he thinks the payments I receive for parenting are enough for us/him to live on. I am soon to find out his goal in life is to sit at home smoking weed all day, dreaming of ways to make money, doing as little as he can.

My life for the next five years resembles the movie *Sleeping with the Enemy*. He has some pretty high expectations given his

---

* Love bombing: showing extreme affection, love, and passion towards someone in a short period of time, in the hopes of winning that person's trust. https://thepopularman.com/love-bombing-definition-signs-resist/

own lack of standards, and I'm good, but not that good. Towels level, socks folded and the labels all facing the correct way. It doesn't sound like much, but this is just the beginning.

Fear of doing wrong. Is it me, why can't I get things right? He's such a nice guy, everyone thinks so, taking the kids and I in, even my dad agrees. Maybe with all he has taken on board and a death in his family it's all been too much. Things will get better, I'll cook his favourite meal and put the kids to bed early.

'Those f__ing kids don't know how to eat properly. I can hear them chewing from over here. It's disgusting.' I don't like the way he's speaking to my children and say so. Bam! his plate goes flying across the room, then he reaches over and takes my plate and starts eating my dinner as if nothing happened. I clean up the mess. It's even on the roof and there's pumpkin and potato sliding down the wall. I look over and see my children silently eating their dinner and my son has tears sliding down his face and he looks up and wipes it away putting on a brave face. My daughter looks mad which is typical of her.

After dinner, he says he hates the sound of chewing it drives him crazy and he's sorry that he did that and he loves me, but it doesn't feel right. No matter how I try and make sense out of what I'm seeing and hearing it just feels wrong. I should have left right then and there, but I love him or, so I think.

The drugs and alcohol have increased, and he is pretty much stoned all the time. I now smoke weed with him because it helps me to sleep. I also start drinking and there are days I drink a lot. So much so that I have lost chunks of my memory. The guilt I feel now over this stage of my life is something I struggle with, because I know my children went through more than I will ever know and for that I am truly sorry.

He's awful every day not just to me but the children as well. I try to leave several times, but he always begs me to come back. 'I love you, it'll be better I promise, you can't live without me, anyway how will you cope?' He slowly chips away at my self-confidence until I get to the point where I don't think I could ever survive without him.

Physically, I'm only a little person and when he gets angry or is trying to get his point across, there's no comparison. He can easily shove me up against a wall when he feels like it. When he does this all I can think is: I'm trapped and where are the kids. Sadly, this 'wall shoving' is becoming the norm.

I'm pregnant, but I don't tell him, but he finds out anyway. I can't remember how, but he tells his family and they are over the moon. I'm now stuck permanently connected to him. I'm in shock, terrified because I know this man is capable of some very bad stuff. I watch his family and you can see they fear him as well.

I'm bathing my son late one afternoon and turn him around to wash his back and what I see makes me physically ill. He has bruising from his lower back to below his little bottom on the tops of his legs. I'm sobbing as I call his mother and she comes around and she sees what has been done to my little boy. I can see the fear and sadness in her face. She begs me not to go to the police and I'm crying because I'm pregnant with her grandchild and I can see she's terrified too. I pack a few things and call my mother. I have no licence or car and I'm reliant on others and they know very little of what's going on because I'm embarrassed and too scared to say anything.

We talk, he's crying and begging me, and I relent. Please don't judge me! I have judged myself much more harshly than you could ever imagine. Upon reflection, I didn't understand my worth. My family saw no worth in me because they kicked me out and my father never visited. My husband rejected me by sleeping with other women, and now this guy thinks I'm useless too, so it must be me, right?

This is as good as it gets and as my dad used to say, 'You made your bed, so lie in it!'

Speaking of beds, I can't sleep in ours anymore. I'm seven months pregnant and he's at me all the time. Life goes on, he won't work anymore or do anything, I'm now living on nothing, he gives me about $60 a week for groceries. I'm taking care of the kids, the house, the gardens, everything. We are walking on glass, literally. I'm trying to keep the children away from him and if he doesn't get his 'hit' I can't control what will happen next.

One good thing, he's not hitting the children anymore. His mother is saying to me that I need to keep the peace and that I'm not to 'set him off'. They were her words. 'He can't help it.' She blames me for all the incidents and I'm SERIOUSLY questioning myself. Can I just say, it's at this point, I think I'm a little crazy! I think I'm forgetting things because he would say, 'Remember, I said …' and when I'd say, 'No you didn't' he would make out he had, and by the hundredth time, I believe I'm a little crazy.

I know I need to leave, but he's lost his brother and I need to hang in there because you can't leave a man when you're about to have his baby and his brother just died. Maybe he is doing all of this because he is mentally exhausted by everything. Now I'm making excuses for him again.

My beautiful baby is born, and he barely visits me in the hospital. I'm not concerned about this. I'm out in under 24 hours anyway. When we get home, he keeps our daughter away from me unless I'm feeding her. I'm too scared to contradict him. I'm feeling extremely defeated now and I just give in. I'm feeding her, and this is one thing he can't control, and I love those beautiful moments when feeding her. She looks up at me and I feel so much love for her. She cries all the time and he's saying it's my fault and it's my milk, so now I don't even have this special feeding moment anymore. She's three months old.

The kids have learnt to stay out of his way and he's too preoccupied by the baby. My two eldest children are sitting with me in the sunshine at the front of the house. My son is on my lap and he's now five years old and we are talking about their father because my eldest daughter is asking questions. My son out of the blue says to me, 'Does that mean he is not my father?' I'm astounded because it has never occurred to me that he thinks the dragon is his father. Somewhere along the way he has forgotten. I reassure him that's not his father, and we chat and cuddle. I'll never forget how that must have felt for him.

My daughter tells me, 'He keeps coming into the bathroom, telling me how to wash myself and I don't like it.' She's nearly ten. I'm watching him now, and I see him doing this, and I tell him to get out. He loses his shit and I cop it, but it's worth it.

That's it, I'm done. I'm thinking to myself, *You can hurt me, but not my kids. You are a disgusting piece of sh__.* Deep down, I'm terrified he might have 'touched' my eldest daughter. I know there is no way he is going to let me leave because he has threatened that if I do, I will never see my youngest daughter again and he will make my life a living hell.

I plan leaving very carefully, and end up giving my kids to my mother – brave move on my behalf, given her history of crazy, but I'm desperate. I don't give her the baby, because he would go batsh__ crazy. I justify this by telling myself he has never hurt her. That afternoon, I tell him it's over. He loses his sh__, smashing the place up, there is glass everywhere, I distract him away from the baby, because he has just laid her down on the floor with smashed glass all around her. So, I head to the kitchen and he pushes me up against the wall and he's screaming at me, right up in my face, then he grabs me by the throat and he's choking me. I can't breathe, but I'm pushing at him and eventually, he lets go, and I start blacking out, then I come around, sitting on the floor.

I get to the lounge and he's dangling the baby by her feet. I'm terrified, he is really looking crazy now pacing around. I've seen this look before and it's not good. I calmly say to him, 'Give me the baby please.' He ignores me. I try again and he's still holding her, and she is crying. The next minute, he throws her, not at me, but I manage to deflect her onto the couch, away from the glass.

This is Day One, and it takes three days to get him out of the house, and I have to do this on my own. I can't even go into what he did to me during those days and nights. I have blanked out much of those three days, but I do remember him finally going on the third day.

I get the locks changed, but he keeps coming around, never calling first, just showing up. I wake up one night and he is standing over my bed watching me sleep. He looks at me and gets into my bed. I'm terrified. This is the type of stalking that continues on and off for two years and it intensifies when I meet someone else.

One day after a child contact visit, he rocks up early to drop our daughter off. I'm a little stronger these days and less likely to fear him by now. I've worked hard at rebuilding my life but what is about to happen changes all that. He kicks in my front door because I'm not home, I'm out with the kids.

I walk into my front yard and say, 'Why did you do that?' pointing to the door. He doesn't say anything that I can hear but punches me to the ground, then proceeds to kick me until I'm crawling on the ground screaming for help. I'm trying to get away from him, as cars drive by and one slows down, but nobody stops to help.

His friend is in the car holding onto our daughter and yells at me that I provoked him. I'm nearly at the door to the house and he is still threatening to kick me. I'm so disorientated now, because he's hit and kicked me in the head so many times, I can't think straight. That's when he says to me in the calmest, nastiest and most calculated voice that I've ever heard, 'I've wanted to do that to you for a very long time.' Even now, when a male becomes menacing towards me, I get this tightening in my gut and I begin to shrink inside looking for a way out. I'm still working on this, because I never want him to have power over me again.

My eldest daughter is in the house and she calls the police which is long overdue and they are useless. They treat me like I did something wrong, and they believe him about me provoking him. They are interviewing me, but I have just been punched and kicked in the head and need an ambulance. They don't call one. They leave, and I'm taken to the hospital and I'm made to wait with every other deadsh__ in the waiting room and I can't stop crying. My mother is with me and she doesn't know what to do or say, so we just sit there, me shrinking further into myself with all these people staring at me.

I feel like the whole world is constantly staring at me now, sad stupid me.

They x-ray me, and I have a fractured eye socket, broken sternum, fractured nose, smashed front teeth, cuts to my forehead, two impending black eyes and a lot of bruising everywhere. He hit me predominantly in the back of my head causing fluid on the brain, which would account for me being so unsteady on my feet. Maybe that's why the police thought I'd been drinking.

A **counsellor** comes and sees me at the hospital and gives me a brochure on domestic violence, then leaves to see someone else. I read the brochure for something to do and it reads like a checklist of my life. The counsellor comes back, and I point to the brochure and she tells me that what has happened to me is domestic violence.

It is at this point I realise it's not me, it's him. This might sound strange but it's true.

I have a headache that just goes on and on and I can't tell you how long I stay hidden in my room. I know people come and I hear lots of whispering, but I don't care because I can't stop crying. I see my dad and he's looking at me saying, 'I'm going to get that bastard!' and I just cry and say, 'Sure dad.' And in my head, I'm screaming *Where the hell were you, all of you, why didn't you help me when I needed you.* I've never felt so alone or so ashamed in my whole life; now everyone knows and I'm horrified.

I get a lawyer and he drafts up the paperwork for the domestic violence restraining order. I keep asking him, while sitting there with makeup covering my bruises, 'Why can't he be charged, he beat me up in front of my children?' He tries to explain to me that they can't because it's not criminal, it's only domestic violence. I'm like, 'What?!'

We go to court and he's right and I'm still in disbelief, I'm trying to focus on the wall because my ex is staring at me. The lawyer comes up to me and says, 'He says you attacked him first and he has applied for a restraining order against you.' What the hell is this? Then I remember his friend and the police. The lawyer says to me, 'Just accept the restraining order and you will get your restraining order.' I want to fight but I have no energy left and I'm trying to hold it together because I don't want him to see me like that. I have no choice, I feel like I'm being punished. I accept my punishment and move on.

It is at that moment I realise this man has a hold on me still. He has been continuing to control me through my fears. Right there and then, I decide he will never know what I'm thinking or feeling again. My success is his failure. I'm going to make something of myself. I will not let him sap my strength and use that to control me ever again. Strangely, once I realise how desperate he is to have control over me I begin to see how vulnerable he is.

A few months later, I notice the kids are in the lounge room and my son is playing cars with his little sister and my eldest daughter is directing them and they are laughing. I grab my camera and they all hug and I get my picture. I still have this picture, because it's the first time I have truly seen them happy in years. I put this picture in a heart-shaped frame beside my bed and it gives me strength that what I'm doing is right for all of us.

It is at this point I start to gain my strength back. I begin to enjoy the little things in life, the sun on my face again, the picnics in the park and hearing the children laugh. I start to do things for myself to gain back my independence. I go to see a movie on my own. I go out for breakfast and a coffee by myself and enjoy the company of a newspaper.

I am back working in a factory and a staff member is being a smarta__ to me, playing at giving me a spanner. I turn around and say to this bloke, 'If you don't give me that now, I'll hit you.' He replies, 'Go on then, hit me!', stabbing his finger at his forehead. The next minute, I punch him, right in the face. *Oh God! I just hit a work colleague.* Well, he looks at me like I have two heads and storms off to the office. The next minute over the loud speaker comes the summons. With trepidation, I enter the office. My boss looks at me and says, 'Don't ever hit the staff again,' and smiles. Relief floods through me and I go back to the machine.

Anger has taken over my life, and I have no way of controlling it. In my head I go over the arguments with the kids, my disdain for my mother and now it is impacting my work. I don't like the person I have become, and it has to stop. I have worked so hard getting my life back together, and now, this!

The **counselling** is great, and I describe it like going to the library. All those bad thoughts are like books you take out and read. When you go back to the library, you chuck them on the return trolley and grab some more. The librarian helps you by putting the books back where they are meant to be, so you can find them if you want and the books are not all mixed up anymore.

I use a band on my wrist and every time I feel angry, I snap myself with the band. I can't remember if this was the counsellor or someone else's idea, but it works. The counselling helps me understand why I'm angry and I stop thinking there is something wrong with me. My anger is directed at all those people around me who never saved me, but how could they? They didn't know and even if they did, would I have left him anyway?

I don't want to work in factories anymore and want a better life for my children and myself. I begin looking at different careers that will provide me financial stability that I will enjoy for the long term and will keep me interested

My kids are getting older and there are children and teens with so many issues at home it's safer for them to live on the streets, so we take in some teenagers at different times.

Then it comes to me: the type of career for me is to keep kids safe. I go back and finish high school and go on to university. I now volunteer with children who are traumatised, because I want to make sure these kids never have to go through what my children or I had to go through, if I can.

Sadly, many women choose to remain with their partners and

lose their children. Violence is not good for any child to be subjected to, let alone to hear it. I work supporting women and children and I work on the front line. For me, it's not about pulling families apart, it's about piecing them back together when it's safe to do so.

I never want to live that way again because my children and I deserve better. So I took this bull by the horns and went and got myself a degree and now I'm earning more than I ever imagined. I take holidays overseas often and bought my first brand new car. I'm saving for my first home and I'm almost there.

Most of all I have learnt to let the anger go, because I've found happiness in doing so. I now smile often, laugh out loud everyday, and be happy. This took a while but it was so worth it.

Go forth, stay safe, and bring on the happiness.

Create your new life with the Six Cs

To create your new life use the **Six Cs.** It starts with **catching a glimpse** of the fun in your life and taking the time to **care for yourself.** Going to **counselling** can help you get out and get in control of your feelings of anger, resentment, loss, remorse and betrayal. By working and being determined to have a **career** and following your career dream through **continued learning** you can create a safe and happy future for you and your children.

CATCH A GLIMPSE: Look at what makes you happy, such as the little things in life, the sun on your face, picnics in the park, hearing the children laugh, watching them have fun playing.

CARE FOR YOURSELF: Do things for yourself to gain back your independence, such as going to see a movie on your own, go out for breakfast, have a coffee by yourself, learn to enjoy your own company and the company of a newspaper.

COUNSELLING: Seeking this type of support is important, as counselling can be the biggest factor that helps a survivor to leave a relationship, and to understand why they feel anger, remorse, and betrayal. It helps you understand why, despite the abuse, you still have a sense of loss for the relationship. It can also help to build up your self-worth, self-respect and self-confidence.

Control your anger: Use a band on your wrist and every time you feel angry, snap yourself with the band. Also seek support from your counsellor with these emotions.

Career guidance: This can help identify your skills and work preferences. It can help foster your ability to access resources and find suitable employment so you can support yourself and your family in the long term. Having a career will create independence, stability and security. This will help to stop the cycle of returning to violence.

Continued education: This has more benefits than you may be aware of. These include developing new and more positive connections with others, gaining new skills, knowledge and understanding. It can provide a sense of purpose, focus and fulfilment. It can improve your self-confidence and you will be modelling positive behaviours for your children. Continued education can help you create and change your life.

© Broken to Brilliant

CHAPTER FOUR

NOTHING CHANGES IF NOTHING CHANGES

'I listened to those that had travelled the road I was about to take. I have the tools I need and will pick up new ones on my journey.'

I LAY IN BED LISTENING TO THE TV BETWEEN MOMENTS OF SUB-conscious sleep. I felt a presence in the room and turned over to see my drunken abuser standing there with a long knife in her hand.

She knew I was trapped. I couldn't make a dash for it if I wanted to. I will always remember the look on her face: pure hatred. Her fingers twitched as she grasped that knife – it was over for me.

In a way, I welcomed death. I was tired – physically, mentally, financially and emotionally drained. Death would bring one thing that I welcomed: peace. I lay back down as I said one last time, 'Leave me alone.' I waited to die, eyes wide, my ears alert to every sound. *Soon it will all be over.*

I waited an eternity, but nothing happened. It took a lot of courage, but I turned over – to see an empty room. She was gone. I slept in the car in the garage, between the back and front seats, hiding on the floor. I had forgotten to take blankets so I was cold, but behind locked doors I felt relatively safe. My heart raced. All I could hear was my shallow breathing as I listened for every sound.

With that knife, the abuse had moved to the next level. The next morning, I drove slowly to the police station. What could I say? Who in their right mind would call the police about their own wife? I started to assemble a sentence. I had to make the police believe me. Outside the police station, I waited a while. I think I was waiting for everyone to leave before I entered as I felt embarrassed asking for help.

When I was eventually called to the front desk, I was so scared I was shaking. I started my sentence, looking the police officer straight in the eye. Halfway through my sentence he said, 'A big burly lad like you, you should be able to look after yourself.'

I didn't know how to answer. I could see on his face he didn't believe me. It didn't matter what I said, he would never believe me.

***

In my car outside the police station, I wondered what I'd said wrong. I realised I was on my own – I had gone to the highest authority in the land and been turned away. I had to go home and find the knife before my abuser came home. (I found it weeks later under the microwave.)

I had already been trying to get help for a long time. I didn't know who to ask, and I had been groomed by my abuser to keep her secret. That was now my burden.

My abuser was making me pay for her uncle's abuse of her as a child. *Direct your abuse at him, not me. It's not my fault.* This person that said they loved me was making me so very unhappy. To avoid going home after work, I would find excuses to do overtime for free or visit my favourite museum. Sometimes I would find myself in a car park, just thinking for hours about what I had gotten myself into, and how I could get out.

My children noticed me change over time. I didn't really listen to them anymore or interact with them like a normal father does, and for that I'm deeply sorry. I had too much on my mind. How could I tell my children what was going on? It would only create side-taking and make a bad situation worse. My abuser was a master of drama creation, always shifting blame.

I was put in hospital with broken glass in my eye needing plastic surgery with multiple operations, followed by a stress-related heart condition and the loss of my business.

A doctor asked me what had happened. I didn't want to lie anymore – it was slowly killing me. So I told him. I told him what was happening at home. I thought, *If I tell the doctor he will get someone to help me.* I waited and waited in my hospital bed, but no-one came.

I tried to talk to my father. He was lost for words. I tried to talk to my mother but she said, 'She's a good girl. It's only a glass of wine with dinner, there's no harm in that.' My abuser had done a really good job of grooming my family over the years, painting a very different picture of who she was, slowly blame-shifting and creating isolation.

I'd had enough. I made plans and moved far away.

For a short time, I experienced freedom. I started to go out, enjoying life.

Then my mum started talking about my abuser coming to live with me. At the airport, I waited for her. I didn't recognise her, she was so thin and drawn. I took her to a hotel to rest, my hopes dashed as she immediately craved that first drink.

But I signed on the dotted line: a 25-year mortgage to put a roof over my abuser's head, knowing I was alone in that debt.

***

An opportunity arose for something positive. I joined a volunteer group and made some friends. One guy asked questions, and as trust grew, I began to share. It was great to talk to someone that did not beat me down but who gave me a voice. It's funny, but it took another friend to tell me my abuser was an alcoholic.

Some of our friends also volunteered there, and one day one of them asked me what was going on at home. When everyone left for the day we stayed behind for a chat with my newfound voice.

That was a bad judgement call on my part. My voice spread to others. As gossip spreads, friends become judges. Before long, that gossip reached my abuser. I paid heavily for breaking the silence. It brought months of escalating abuse. She started to spread word that I was a child abuser. I never did recover from that lie – it didn't make any difference to show the proof I was certified to work with children. I was guilty as charged.

I moved on to volunteer somewhere else, in a group that was out of reach of my abuser but always in fear that one day she would start to destroy that, too.

***

Out of the blue, my abuser suggested going to marriage guidance counselling. I agreed pretty quick – but not just marriage guidance, she needed rape counselling. Hope at last!

We had couples counselling, then individual counselling. I really enjoyed it. Of course, my abuser started to lie when asked questions like, 'How much do you drink? Have you had extra-marital relationships?'

As hostilities grew in the home, the counsellor set up 'safe areas'. I had my bedroom, another room and the back garden, where I spent much of my time. If friends visited they were sent to me in the garden.

Safe areas had rules: no drinking, no rows, no shouting, no hitting, and I could report back if these rules were broken. My abuser hated that for the first time she was being held accountable for her actions.

The counsellor explained that I was not only the white knight trying to rescue my abuser, I was also the second rape victim in the relationship.

To begin my recovery, the counsellor asked me to choose a point in time before I met my abuser when I was happiest. For me, it was my teenage years when I was making model aeroplanes, so I picked 15 years of age. My abuser called me a child abuser for picking 15 years of age, but in reality I just had a happy childhood, something my abuser hated and wanted to dismantle.

The counsellor suggested I buy model aeroplane kits and try to recreate the feelings I had before the abuse. My first model was a mess, so I built a second, which didn't look much better. But for the first time, I no longer had my abuser taking up so much space in my head. A small fraction was now dedicated to recovering what I had lost during the years of dismantlement.

I made new friends. I started to go out. I entered model-making competitions and even won prizes. It gave me back a part of me that was taken away.

For my abuser it was a different story. She didn't want to recover but to blame-shift rather than address her own past years of trauma as a child. She started gossiping to others that I spent all my time making models, and was careful not to explain that it was a task set by the counsellor. Sometimes I would come home to find a model on the floor, crushed. She tried her hardest to distract me from my progress.

My abuser's drinking and violence increased at home. One day, I walked out of my 'safe area' and she pushed me against the wall. Her hands were around my throat as she said, 'Hit me! Hit me! Then I can tell the police.' I kept my hands at my sides although I was struggling for breath, not wanting to give her any excuse to call the police – not realising I could have called them. It's amazing how strong she was when she was drunk. I didn't want to give her an excuse to call the police, so I had to let the attack run its course – something that I had become used to by now.

Near the end of my 'discovery year', I lost my job, because my boss could see my mind was elsewhere. Sooner after, my abuser went on holiday. My first port of call was my doctor – he was great. I told him what was happening at home and he instantly put me on a health care plan with blood tests and my heart monitored. The results weren't good. I now realised that this dysfunctional relationship was having a negative impact on my health as well.

He advised me to contact the mental health authorities immediately to see if they could help with my abuser. As soon as I got outside, I rang them, only to be told, 'I wish we could help, but we can't.' I went home in shock.

A few days later I tried ringing them again. Apparently, my abuser could voluntarily admit herself for a mental health assessment. *That's not going to happen.* Or I could ring for help when I was being attacked – so they could witness it and remove her.

Do you realise how difficult it is to ring for help when you're being attacked? I did try, only to have my phone forcibly removed and thrown to the other side of the room.

Then they said changes to the law meant that my abuser had 'rights' … so where were mine?? That was the end of my dealings with the mental health authorities.

***

In the early hours one morning, I was awakened by my dogs barking. Someone was trying to get in to my home! I raced to the door – to find my abuser walking in. I discovered she would often get up early in the morning and walk the streets in search of alcohol.

I didn't know where to turn for help. Confused, I found the number for Alcoholics Anonymous. A nice guy explained what an alcoholic was. He asked me how much my abuser drank. I said, 'A half to a full bottle of vodka each night.'

I was invited to attend a meeting. I arrived early, all dressed up and ready to go. I wanted to cure her alcoholism.

Everyone was given a chance to talk. As I listened I could identify with what each person was going through. Finally, I was alone no more.

I never talked, and at one meeting I was approached and asked why I came. I said, 'I live with an alcoholic and I came here for the cure so I could take it home and give it to my abuser. I assume it's tablets.'

She gave a little laugh and said, 'No, there's no tablets. There's no instant cure. We come here to learn about alcoholism and the Twelve Steps of recovery.' I sat in my car for a while after the meeting and cried, but I kept going to meetings.

I became a member of Al-Anon – an organisation set up to help friends and family members recover from the effects of living with an alcoholic. I felt at home in those meetings. I attended up to four meetings a week and made many friends.

When I eventually did start to share at a meeting, it was full of anger – it was about my abuser. It was about her, week after week. But then something changed as I started to understand Step One: we admit we are powerless over alcohol and that our lives have become unmanageable.

Then I began to speak about me and what I was doing in my recovery and what I was learning and how my life had changed in the program.

I had two sponsors – one from Al-Anon and one from Alcoholics Anonymous. They helped me understand my past and what had happened to me, and we discussed my future. They made me see that 'nothing changes if nothing changes'. I discovered how I had neglected my gut instinct over time, convincing myself it would be okay. I now had the power to say 'no' and to seek help. To learn to detach from the alcoholic and alcoholism. To hand back her secret.

It wasn't the Twelve Steps that saved my life – they are just words on a piece of paper. It was a man and a woman that saved my life – my sponsors – simply because they had the Twelve Steps carved into their lives and I wanted to be like them.

Life at home had become unbearable. But now I had the option to remove myself and no longer be a witness. My home was now the topic of gossip in the street. Someone even said, 'All we hear is her screaming. We never hear you.'

My new friends in Al-Anon could not be groomed by my abuser – a small blessing. My new friends where I volunteered could not be groomed by my abuser – another small blessing. I took confidence from these small victories.

If the car broke, I no longer panicked to fix it. When my abuser damaged her room, I walked away, it wasn't my business. If she broke a window I said, 'That's ok, that will be $12 please,' and got it fixed. For the first time, I started to enjoy my life by changing the way I thought.

Yes, it's a very long journey fraught with danger, but I was learning new boundaries that I never had before.

***

The night my abuser was removed began quietly – a pleasant change. It was cold outside, so I moved from the garden to the kitchen to do my models. I was minding my own business when my abuser shouted that her friend was coming over to get me. I went to the next room where she was on the phone in the dark. I asked, 'Why? What have I done?'

She said, 'She's coming over with her husband to beat you up.'

I panicked and called the police. My abuser was on triple-distilled vodka that night, a gift from one of her friends. I recorded everything on my phone as evidence in case I needed it, as I had been doing before.

Time passed and no police, so I called again. I was outside now. The police said to stay where I was, they were on their way. It was so cold I had to get my coat. While I was inside, my abuser's friends turned up, and she went outside to meet them. I locked the doors and windows. I was relatively safe. Finally, the police arrived.

It was two in the morning by the time she was removed with her friends, taking a bag of clothes I'd gathered for her. The police recommended I go to the courthouse the next morning to get an interim domestic violence restraining order.

I was the first one at the court. I got the paperwork but I have reading difficulties, so I asked for help but no-one was available. I sat in McDonald's with a cup of tea to have a go. I got stuck with some words, so I asked a lady next to me – she was great. In no time, I had the paperwork filled out, mistakes and spelling errors included.

When my name was finally called the court was almost empty. I sat in front of the judge as he read my statement, looking over the top of his glasses every so often. I was nervous and questioning myself. Had I stuffed up the paperwork? If I had, she would be allowed back.

Then he said, 'You have been through a lot, haven't you? I will grant this order.' Well, I just broke down, my head in my hands as the tears flowed.

The judge said, 'Why are you upset? It's what you wanted isn't it?'

I said, 'Yes, I just thought you wouldn't believe me.'

Then he said the best words ever: 'Why wouldn't I believe you? It's the truth isn't it?'

***

At home, still in a daze, I phoned friends. I was so happy. Then I walked around the house. It was quiet. I checked every room just in case. By the end of the night I was back at my table making a model with a cup of tea, but the deadly quiet was deafening.

I didn't really sleep that night. I was still listening, straining to hear something.

The next day I changed the locks.

A few days later, I came home, opened the door, and there she was. Struck by immediate fear I walked outside and called the police. 'She's back.'

They were pretty quick, less than ten minutes, but they couldn't remove her. She hadn't yet been served with the court order. *Really?*

I was in contact with the police every day for the next two weeks, as they tried to catch her at work or at home to deliver the court order.

That was the most fearful time. If she was in the house I would leave, trying to protect myself at all times.

Then one day I came home and the house was empty though her car was on the driveway. I searched the house one room at a time. I even opened wardrobes just to check. Then it dawned on me: the police must have finally delivered the court order.

I was so relieved, I was joyful and heartbroken at the same

time – tired, stressed, full of anxiety and very mentally unwell. It took several weeks for me to fully believe she was gone. At night, I lay in bed still listening and still waiting.

I had to go to court several times. She had a witness; I had my sponsor from Al-Anon for support. The judge looked at both statements, confused, and said, 'There are two statements here. Both are very different. Which one should I believe?'

Like a little schoolboy, I put up my hand. 'Mine,' I said.

The judge said, 'And why's that?'

I took my phone from my pocket and said, 'My statement was taken from evidence from my phone recording, so I would like to submit my phone as evidence.' With that, my abuser's statement was dismissed. I had won another small victory.

My abuser's solicitor wanted me to attend arbitration, but I wasn't interested. My abuser made promises, but I was over her promises.

I had to gather evidence of domestic violence and abuse. It's amazing when you start looking how much evidence you can find. I had a friend help me – she was amazing, she knew how to document and present everything. By the end of it, we had a book of evidence to give the court. Due to the severity of the case and the long-term abuse, the judge ordered a ten-year domestic violence order, but my abuser had already left the country. She knew what was going to happen – the police later issued warrants for her arrest.

***

Years of abuse had taken its toll on me, not only mentally and emotionally but physically, financially and spiritually. I had three stress-related heart attacks, my health was failing, even breathing brought pain. I was put on medication which I must take for the rest of my life, and old injuries still give pain – reminders of a past that once was.

My doctor sent me to see a specialist in neurophysiology for victims of domestic violence. It took me a long time to start talking – talking brought fear. But slowly, I did talk. Fear was replaced with confidence. Everything I said was documented – that too brought fear. He diagnosed me with Complex Post-Traumatic Stress Disorder (C-PTSD).* I was set tasks and given diagrams to help me understand my mental state during abuse. Then, he told me how my brain had adapted to situations and why fear ruled my life. I had no self-confidence, very little self–esteem. I had been dismantled and isolated.

Life after abuse has been hard, nothing short of a bl__dy nightmare. There's been highs and lows, achievements and losses. A constant learning and relearning curve called life after abuse. I listened to those that had travelled the road I was about to take and it was full of potholes, but there was no rush now.

I did struggle for a long time. I had been abused for so long that abuse was normal now. I moved my little TV into the kitchen to bring in some kind of noise to end the silence of quiet. This new world people called freedom was more scary than before. I would sometimes sit on the floor all curled up for hours, rocking, just waiting for something. Friends would visit but couldn't find me – I would be hiding away, somewhere dark maybe, sleeping.

My best buds, Al-Anon friends and my church friends, they

---

* Complex PTSD describes the symptoms of long-term trauma (months or years) where the person feels they cannot escape. It is distinct from PTSD in that it distorts a person's core identity.

were fantastic. They asked if they could help and they did. We set about cleaning my home, doing repairs long forgotten about, throwing things out, sending my abuser's belongings to charity shops – brand new clothes by the bagful with the price tag still on that I got her, now discarded.

Her bedroom was stripped and repainted, the smell of booze and cigarettes replaced with fresh paint. Everything was bleached. The smell of eucalyptus started to fill the air. Lawns were cut and plants moved in. A car dumped out the front was moved and worked on, being brought back to life – it, too, a victim of abuse. It's just amazing how many people you meet on their journey, that can help you on your journey.

Old friends that were unhealthy were cut free and in time replaced with new friends who made no inappropriate demands. I ate more healthily and exercised daily. I cherished my dogs, my buddies that shared in my story. It was so different than before – we would walk for miles. Living again has been an experience – some of it good, some bad – but there's always something new to explore around the corner.

It's been exhausting. Sometimes I'd think throwing in the towel would be so much simpler than the test put before me today, but I'd get up the next day and start again.

Sometimes, I just have the need to escape and have time where I can enjoy peace, away from reality. Me and my boys (dogs) just get in the car and drive, sometimes for days if not weeks, visiting new places and taking photographs on our journey. We're on our walkabout. When my empathy for others is exploited, a sign from my gut says, 'We have done this before. It's cyclic. Say no!'

I found my higher power – a God of my understanding – and gave him things I could no longer handle for safekeeping until I am ready to take them back. He never stops helping me.

***

Friends asked me, 'You're free now. How does it feel?'

I often pondered that question. Yes, I was free on paper, but how did I feel? Void, I think. I didn't expect to feel this way because I had won the war. However, like any soldier that celebrates when peace is finally declared, when the war finally finishes and they go home to close their bloodshot eyes, they are revisited by past conflicts, with a question next morning: am I really free? Is this really freedom?

This is the freedom I experience every day now. I can get in my car and drive miles just for that one photo of an empty beach. I can go to sleep and say, 'I don't want to dream about you tonight. I want to dream about places I've visited.' I can take my dogs for a walk for no particular reason at all. I can go into a shop just to look, even those shops that were out of bounds before. I enjoy the simple things in life. A cup of tea never tasted so good, especially with a chocolate biscuit.

Sometimes, I'm asked if I had my life over would I go through it again. Not on your life!

Before I met my abuser, I had life dreams, aspirations, a wish to succeed in a job I loved, to enjoy my hobbies and time with my family. Yet my empathy for another was abused, taken, destroyed in front of my very eyes and I did nothing – I was powerless. My abuser took what didn't belong to her: my life and my life with my children. The sole aim was to protect her childhood abusers and her shame as a victim.

My aims in life have changed. My abuser in her own way taught me a lot that I need to pass on to others trapped in the silent cycle of abuse. To outreach my hand and say, 'Hold tight, we're going for a ride.'

I'm an avid speaker about domestic violence now. If I can help, I will. Many are benefiting from my experiences with my abuser, so not all was lost in that bl__dy war.

It's five years since she was removed. I've been in the newspapers and spoken on radio. I still attend Al-Anon meetings. I was invited to speak at a seminar where I met the founder of the charity Broken to Brilliant. This led me to a workshop to write this chapter, where I met 11 other brave souls like me, each one with a personal story.

The best thing of all is that I have a family now. This family does not judge or gossip, it doesn't criticise, it doesn't put me down like my blood family do. It reminds me of times before I knew my abuser, when times were good. This family gives unconditional love. They're proud of me, have been with me through thick and thin. My Al-Anon family and my survivor family are always there for me.

Fear is still my companion and I still have some deep-seated issues locked away in a box covered with a dusty sheet, but in time they will be addressed. I know I still have a lot to learn about saying no to unacceptable behaviour. I'm picking up the pieces of dismantlement, and realise it will take time. But I'm in no rush. I have the tools now and am sure I will pick up new ones on my journey.

CHALLENGES

There are many **CHALLENGES** you will face in your journey of recovery. You may feel like giving up, but don't. It is worth working through these **CHALLENGES** to rebuild your life, to feel free and to be triumphant.

CONDEMN UNACCEPTABLE BEHAVIOUR: Offensive, belittling, abusive or threatening behaviour to another is not acceptable. Do not allow people to treat you badly. Learn the tools to be able to say, 'No.' Learn how to set your boundaries.

HEALTHY HABITS: A habit is something that is a routine for you, something you will repeat, often without knowing it. When you create healthy habits, it can help with your mental health and wellbeing. Set small goals. Know your triggers. Take time to stop, to rest, to go out and about to clear your mind. Eat healthy food.

ATTEND COUNSELLING: Counselling can help you to understand what you are experiencing and give you strategies to address the situation. They may set you tasks and ask you to reflect on these – for example, to do something you love or to set a boundary. This will help you move through the challenging times.

LEARN: There is a constant learning and relearning curve called life. You will realise you have a lot to learn to help you move through your recovery journey. Attend a support group, do the tasks and activities suggested, follow the steps in this book, learn the warning signs, set boundaries, and take time for self-care.

LOVE AGAIN: Allow some time before you dive into another relationship. Work on yourself through counselling and learn as much as you can. When you have formed new healthy habits, then you can take the chance to love again.

EMPATHY: Empathy is the ability to understand another person's experience, perspective and feelings. This is an important skill to have, but don't confuse empathy with making people happy or being nice. If you are too empathetic you may need to learn to set boundaries, so people do not take advantage of you.

NOTICE EARLY WARNING SIGNS: Does your partner make you feel uncomfortable or afraid, put you down, make fun of you, make you feel worthless, stop you from seeing your own friends or family, tell other people you make things up and easily get confused, threaten you, scare or hurt you by being violent e.g. hitting, choking, smashing things? Seek help if you notice any of these signs.

GENUINE FRIENDS: Kindly cut away from toxic people and unhealthy relationships – these are the relationships that make you feel uncomfortable, sad and afraid. Healthy relationships are respectful. They enrich you, make you the best person you can be, and you will feel joy. Genuine friends step forward when times get tough. They dig in and help to support you – you will know who they are.

Exercise daily: Take long walks each day and express gratitude for what has gone well in your day. Outdoor walking has a range of health benefits including reducing blood pressure, body fat, total cholesterol and risk of depression. Hippocrates said, 'Walking is man's best medicine.'

Seek peace and enjoy life: Take the time to get away, where you can enjoy peace and do activities that bring you joy. Find your higher power – this does not have to be a religion, it can be spiritual, a connection with all living things, the universe, regardless of what a higher power is to you, having faith in a higher power can help you rebuild your life.

CHAPTER FIVE

I BELIEVE IN ME

'I believe and love me. I trust me to live true to myself and to others. I AM ME!'

As I walked across the field to collect my children from school, I had no idea how real the fear of loss felt. I was about to find out.

I passed a classroom, watching all the students stream out around me. As I rounded a corner, a frantic school officer met me. 'He's on the school grounds!'

My eldest child was safe – the classroom teacher had recognised my husband in time to remove the child to a safe, windowless room. But where was my youngest child? No-one had seen my youngest leave the classroom. My child wasn't standing in the meeting place outside the classroom – the spot we had agreed on, next to the plants.

I froze, paralysed by fear. I cried. I shook. I couldn't breathe. I couldn't understand what was being said to me.

The principal led me to an area where we could talk. My husband had verbally abused her in front of other parents and she was visibly shaken. Others did not normally see this side of him; this was kept for me.

***

At the very end of my marriage, I had been granted a restraining order. My husband had finally been evicted from the house and couldn't come within a few hundred metres of me. I had been back to court for restraining orders to safeguard the children, but we were still waiting for those to be issued. In the meantime, I had been taking comfort from the fact that he wouldn't enter the school grounds while I was there – thinking that he would not attempt to break the law.

I continued to work near my children's school. This enabled me to walk with them every morning and afternoon, all three of us being on hyper-alert just in case we saw him.

***

I was led to the quiet room with no windows. I still cannot put into words the relief of seeing both my children there. They were shaking, disorientated and crying. This was their father that had caused a school to go into lockdown, something they had only ever seen done as a practice during the school day.

We stayed in that room for some time. He kept coming back and finding the principal to give her a piece of his mind. The police couldn't find him on or off the school premises. He kept returning and disappearing until someone took it upon themselves to take us home. They had to lead me – I was unable to make that decision for myself.

After the divorce, I was very lucky when my ex-husband left the country, but I never really knew if he would return again and just show up. I contacted airport security and the special police force to find out if they could let me know if he did enter the country. No, they couldn't, as it was a breach of his privacy!

I lived in a 'just in case' fear. My eyes would play tricks on me. I saw him at the supermarket, driving his car or just walking on a path.

Panic attacks and fear of loss still impact me today. I have taken medication to help with the panic attacks and learnt how to breathe, how to think clearly and how to focus myself away from what is causing the panic.

The fear of loss is very real and will never leave me. Fear that lies and deception will take my children away from me – the fear of death. Fear I control by believing that I have taught the children well, that their minds are able to work out right from wrong.

If I find myself lost, I breathe and believe in me.

***

If I think back, it took me a lifetime to leave him. I knew a very long time ago we would not grow old together, but I didn't realise I would be leaving a domestic-violence marriage.

I decided I had had enough after a friend confirmed that my marriage was not normal. Why did I not know?

She asked me one evening, 'Do you feel safe in your marriage?' I had trouble answering her honestly, and she took a chance that she was right. She showed me a speech she had given to an audience of domestic violence survivors. She was a survivor and she knew what to look for.

Although I was not being physically hit, I was living a life of domestic bullying and abuse. Acknowledging to myself that this was domestic violence was a shocking realisation!

Being told 'You're stupid', 'You're thick', being compared to a dustbin, feeling useless. 'You're not someone that should have had children as you are so incapable.' Being loaded with blame when your husband has made the wrong decision, but of course, it was not his fault! 'The gravy is too runny. Why can't you just make gravy properly?' 'You can't even make a custard, it's too thick!' 'Don't put so much pickle in my sandwich.' 'Put more pickle in my sandwich.' 'Can't you do anything right? You know how I like things!'

He once stopped eating for a week. He told me I had made him want to die. This was so distressing for me, and I found it difficult to conceal from the children. They were fully aware something was very wrong.

One afternoon while he lay in his filthy bed, he delivered a torrent of verbal abuse. Every sentence started with the word 'YOU'. I lost myself in a red haze. I punched him in the chest while crying and shouting at him. I grabbed his shirt and twisted it around my hand so that it tightened on his neck. I wanted him to die, to release me from what he was doing to me.

All the while, he just lay there looking at me with that look. Mocking me. Pitying me as I displayed the 'crazy lady' he said I was. The haze disappeared. I left the house to calm down – this wasn't me! This action was later used against me – I was the nutty one, not him!

I found help for him. A couple of male counsellors came to visit him. This aggravated him more. He told them what he thought they wanted to hear and sent them on their way.

I tried and tried, always living in fear of his aggressive nature when I made a mistake. It would start with him bouncing on his toes. This could go on for days until the explosion. Then the verbal abuse would start. Shouting, swearing, blaming, getting in my face so close that I could feel his spittle as it left his mouth. Too scared to wipe it off my face in case I provoked him further. Watching him clench and unclench his hands into fists. Watching his jaw jut forward and his shoulders push back to make his chest look larger. Watching as his biceps flexed and the toe bouncing increased to the point where his heels didn't touch the ground.

Then came the blame. 'You made me react like this.' 'You make me behave like this.' 'You don't try.' 'You make me lose my temper.' 'You never listen to me.'

Throwing anything that was close to hand: books, shovels, clothing. Close enough to cause a draft but never close enough to actually hit me. Ripping his clothes off and throwing them at me because I made him lose his temper. Punching holes in walls and doors. Ripping fixtures off a wall. Always so close to me, but never touching me.

Being driven with my children at unsafe speeds as he hurled abuse. If I drove, continually being told I was 'sh__ at driving'. Having my ears blasted as he turned to shout at the children in the back of the car if they got too excited and made too much noise, which was probably every time we travelled as a family.

Not being allowed to listen to the radio at an audible volume. Reducing my hours of work to be able to look after him and the children. Being continually told how important he and his job were, how they needed him to work the overtime. Therefore, why did I work? I didn't earn much.

One afternoon when I was working late, I received a phone call from our home number but was unable to take it. After the third call, I answered, only to hear my eldest child whispering down the phone. 'Where are you, Mum? Dad's going mad and shouting. I'm hiding under my bed. I have to go. He's calling me and he can't find me.' I couldn't get home quick enough. I had to save the children!

He was sitting at the kitchen table waiting for me. He followed me around the house, continuing with the verbal abuse. In the loungeroom in front of the TV I found my youngest child, who had developed an amazing act of becoming invisible – shrinking into the chair, becoming so still and quiet.

One morning, I heard a noise from the kitchen that I couldn't recognise. I found the children in the walk-in pantry, using a bread knife to enlarge a hole in the door – a hole made when my husband headbutted it while in a mood with me. Their dad had developed the art of suddenly appearing behind you, and they wanted to be able to tell where he was. 'We want to know if Dad is in the pantry hiding, and we want to see him coming when we are in there getting food.'

***

The deciding moment for me was the last time he ever threw anything at me. The children were having something to eat before they went to bed. The three of us were standing in the kitchen next to the breakfast bar. He appeared with a plastering tool in his hand. Foul language came from his mouth. 'You're a f__ing b___d c__t. Everything is always your f__ing fault. This is bull__.'

He threw the plastering tool at me. Again it missed and hit the wall, but the intent was there as it flew past me.

My eldest child shouted, 'Don't throw things at my mum!' My youngest stood still and tried to become invisible again.

I calmly put the children to bed. I tried not to let them see my distress that they had to witness that. I tried to hide my anger that their dad thought it was okay to behave like that in front of children.

I found his keys and got him a spare pair of underpants. I told him to leave. Of course, he didn't and wouldn't, but I kept trying. I tried to push him to the door. 'Just go,' I said. 'Just f__ off. You can't say that to me. Leave. Just leave me alone.'

Of course, I couldn't actually move him. He was a lot bigger than me and so much stronger. I found myself digging my nails into his stomach in fear and desperation. I had no choice but to give up as he stood there silently mocking me.

The first thing I had to do was admit to myself my situation and face my fears. I had to face the fear that he would increase the abuse 100%. I had to act. I phoned the women's helpline numbers I had been given by my friend. I have no idea how I did it, and I have no idea how anyone understood this blubbering wreck of a woman who made the calls, but somehow, they knew what to say and how to guide me. They told me to make my safety plan, find my important documents and hide them, and get some money in my wallet. These phone calls reinforced what I knew and somehow gave me the strength to go through with it.

My next port of call was to find a lawyer. Again, I took the advice of a friend. Again, it took all my courage to place the call, make an appointment and go through with it. It would have been so much easier to stay with him. I took two friends with me to the appointment but I managed to sit in the lawyer's office by myself. Again, I was a blubbering wreck and I'm sure I didn't make very much sense at all through the tears and snot. They advised me to seek a restraining order, told me the process I needed to go through, told me again to make a safety plan. I knew I was going to leave him.

I then had to go to the police and again disclose to complete strangers all the personal details that previously I had told no-one about. The police advised that I needed a restraining order in place to actually remove him from the house! This scared the life out of me. I was overcome with fear about what he could do to me and the children – the threats he might carry out.

I went to the courts, filled out the necessary documents and submitted them. I then had to wait a few weeks before the court could fit me in for a hearing. Meanwhile, at home the verbal abuse was amping up. I moved out of the marital bedroom and alternated between my children's bedrooms. Eventually, I and both of the children slept in the same room. We all felt safer that way.

My court date came round. When I entered the courtroom I could feel the look the judge gave me: another woman crying 'domestic violence'. Once he started to ask who I was and I couldn't even say my own name, he visibly softened. He asked his questions, listened to me, and on the same day granted the restraining order.

I had to wait for the order to be served by the police, which felt like another lifetime. The day they served the order, I took the children to the park until I got the all clear that he had been removed from the property and had driven away.

The three of us returned home to an eerie house that had been ransacked as he gathered his bits and pieces. Temporary accommodation leaflets were strewn all over the floor. I broke down with grief. This was how I had had to end my marriage.

That very same evening he came to the door to abuse me through the security door. By the time the police arrived, he had disappeared.

A few days later, he used his key to enter the property. I tried to stay away from him but he followed me through the house, telling me I had killed him and he had tried to take his own life in the car. The police arrived with police dogs and squad cars. He was totally unhinged and told the police what a c__t I was, as well as other names. He was asked to leave his keys and was taken off the property, driven straight to the hospital and put under police guard and on suicide watch.

The next day I found three suicide notes – one to each child and one to his mother, telling her not to trust me. In the car boot I found a packet of very large black bin liners and a leather belt.

I don't look back on my marriage and ponder or ask why. I don't question his actions or my responses or reminisce over the good or bad times. I feel no pity for him or myself, or bitterness towards him or sadness for the loss of time.

Maybe I should thank him for the person I have become since he has been gone. Seeing myself for the person I really am and having the new-found confidence to be that person. Seeing life in the positive not the negative, and enjoying every day.

I don't and never will look backward, only forward.

***

I did not know, as I didn't confide in anyone, that I was being abused. By the end of my marriage, I had no self-esteem or confidence. I was unable to make decisions by myself. I was just waiting for his next outburst and the next bout of self-loathing and uselessness I would feel.

My main support person was the friend that helped me take a look at my marriage. She was able to guide me through some of the legal processes of lawyers, and she gave me an alternative way to look at things. She advised which counsellor I could phone for therapy. She was always at the end of the phone line for me. She took time off work to accompany me to a couple of court dates. She was also prepared to look after all of the important documents I had been advised to gather and remove from the marital home.

My work was very supportive up to a point. I was able to take time off at short notice – for court dates and if I needed to support the children or have a day to myself trying to get my thoughts in order. The only time they were not good to me was when I turned up to work crying. My husband had stolen $20,000 from the bank account attached to the mortgage. I was told if I couldn't stop the flow of tears and be professional, I should go home. I controlled myself, and that was the start of me gaining control of my thoughts and emotions.

I found counselling support that was exactly what I and the children needed when we were going through all the changes. The children had their own counsellor and I went to the woman's group. I found this incredibly hard to start with. It took me at least two weeks before I actually spoke. Over the next few weeks, my courage grew and I spoke more and more about what had happened to me over the years. Through this group, I discovered so many things that had gone on that were so wrong in so many ways. The man was a monster! I was re-finding my strength.

The rest I did on my own and with self-reflection. I started to listen to myself, trust my thoughts and compare past and current behaviours. I began to notice it was not me!

I have learnt over the last few years to believe in myself and my angels, and to be kind to my soul.

I have done a huge amount of self-reflection. To some degree, I have stopped being manipulated by others for their personal gain. I have learnt how to put boundaries in place without feeling guilty about it. I have discovered it's those that take from you who don't like the boundaries you put in place. I then leave them to their thoughts and go my own way.

I have taught myself to like myself again. To look in the mirror and like who looks back at me! I can now trust myself to make decisions, whereas before, I was always so wrong from the perception of my ex-husband, or blamed if things went wrong.

I am able to not get upset if anyone is rude or short-tempered with me. I just have a personal thought that maybe they are having a bad day and I am the person they can be negative with. Or maybe they are in a situation that has them behaving in such a manner.

I find myself incredibly happy with life. I can feel the smile on my face most of the time now. I have challenged myself to a lifelong ambition, and I now ride a motorbike with the biggest cheesy grin ever!

I have learnt that perception and reflection go hand in hand! I have changed my behaviours accordingly, knowing I am not useless or to blame. I am me. You will have to like me as I am.

I changed my outlook on life completely. I now know being positive brings more positivity into your life. Being a good person and kind to yourself brings more good things.

I moved from the marital home, away from all the bad memories and feelings that took over when I was in that house. Away from the places I couldn't sit with my back to. I took my time to find the house that would be a real home for me and the children, the house that would make me feel at peace. I redecorated the whole house for sale and laid new floors, and this is where my belief in myself really took hold.

A friend kept telling me how strong I was, but I couldn't understand why she would say that. Now though, being so happy in my new home, my children happy too, managing the mortgage, bills and general running of the house, working full-time, having a social life and riding my bike, I am on top of the world! I am strong!

Time has helped me heal as well. Through self-reflection I have developed an understanding of how I was brought up, the way this shaped my life – looking for what I felt I didn't have as a child, looking for love.

Nobody is putting me down constantly. I don't hear the word 'you' starting every sentence. My opinion matters and counts for something, I am listened to and able to express myself without fear. I don't walk on eggshells. I don't have to judge the mood before I speak. I don't have to do things I don't want to, or lie to protect the children.

I can see my friends and have the people I want in my life.

I believe in myself. What I have achieved and what I can still achieve. I know the truth. I know how to treat others and how I want to be treated myself. I am the only one who will look after me.

I sleep well and soon I won't need the medication for anxiety. I no longer suffer from irritable bowel syndrome on a weekly basis. It only flares up when I make the wrong choice with food. If I feel under pressure, I control how much and what I eat until the moment has passed.

Since breaking free I am rewiring my brain and regaining my self-worth. I have changed my outlook on life. My children and I are happy in our new home. I have a fulfilling life with my family, friends, work and enjoying my passions – riding free.

I believe and love me, I trust me to live true to myself and to others. I AM ME!

This process COMBATS low self-esteem

I am on top of the world! I am strong because I have been able to develop a process which COMBATS my lack of confidence and self-esteem. I have taken these steps to develop my courage and confidence, and my belief and trust in myself.

COUNSELLING: Seek support through counselling services. The children had their own individual counsellor and I attended a women's group.

OUTLOOK: Change your outlook on life completely. Quieten the little voice inside your head. Refocus your attention to being a good person and being kind to yourself. Being more positive brings more positivity into your life and it also brings more good things.

MOVE: Move away from the marital home. Move away from all the bad memories and feelings that can overtake you. Move away from the places that have the memories.

BOUNDARIES: Learn how to set boundaries. Know your own limits. It is okay to say no without feeling guilty. You can be assertive.

ALTERNATIVE VIEW: Seek an alternative view – from lawyers, the police, counsellors, domestic violence services, a trusted friend – to help you see clearly and take action.

TIME: It will take time to heal. Allow yourself this time. Take time to self-reflect. Take time to look after yourself – self-care.

Self-reflection: Take the time to do healthy self-reflection. Don't look back. Stop the blame game. Do not beat up on yourself or get stuck in the 'poor me' mindset. Identify what upsets or triggers you. Address each issue one at a time and develop a different outlook on it. Change how you react or respond.

© Broken to Brilliant

CHAPTER SIX

WITHOUT APOLOGY

*'I am brave, I am beautiful, I am strong,
I am capable and I am worthy.'*

ONE AFTERNOON WE WERE HAVING A HANDSTAND COMPETITION in the local park, laughing side by side, seeing who could stay upside down the longest. I was 19 and he was 20 – an active, happy young couple.

He began to get irritated with my better technique and the mood changed. I offered to help by holding his legs while he practised.

Suddenly and without warning, as I supported him, he lashed out and kicked me in the head. I fell to the ground with the force of the blow. He looked at me, turned his back and strode home.

I was left sitting in the grass, crying in pain, wondering what had just happened. After a little while I walked back home too. I tried to speak with him about it, but he said that nothing had happened, I was imagining it and just starting an argument. 'It was nothing like that. You were the one who walked into me,' he seethed, before refusing to speak to me for hours. In tears, I realised that he must be right.

I apologised to him.

***

The scarce episodes of physical violence I experienced from him pale into insignificance compared to the constant, insidious and undetected emotional sabotage that I endured for over 20 years. His campaign was calculated and quiet and happened so slowly that I was blinded to the crippling effects on my self-esteem, confidence and decision-making.

As an educated and successful woman I have a position of authority and influence in my career and am very well respected by my colleagues, yet I missed the early signs. I failed to see what was happening to me. And so did everyone else.

In those early dating months, he presented me with roses, bought me clothes and jewellery, wrote me love letters and was the perfect boyfriend. I fell in love quickly and deeply with this amazing man. In fact, everyone loved him because he was such a great guy. So when he asked if I was really going to wear that outfit, or he got upset if I wasn't wearing the ring he had bought me, I thought it was because he loved me with his whole heart too. Now I realise it was his way of beginning to control my thoughts, my beliefs and my actions.

I was asleep to the early indicators of domestic abuse. I had no warning system in place. Like the smoke from a fire that silently seeps its way under the gap of a closed door, his narcissistic control over me was just as gradual, dangerous and intense.

***

One day we were driving past a salon and I mentioned that I hadn't been to a hairdresser for a long time. That was my way of asking his permission to get my hair cut because subconsciously I knew that everything needed to be his idea and under his control. He suggested that I book an appointment, but I double-checked with him several times as I didn't want to inconvenience his day. I had my hair cut but asked to skip the blow dry so that I could get back home without delay.

'Your hair looks nice,' he said. 'I hope that putting your looks in front of the family that you claim to love was worth it.' Then he loaded the kids into the car and drove off without telling me where he was going or for how long. He wouldn't answer his phone.

Hours later, he returned and I was visibly distressed but he disgustedly told me not to let the kids see me like that because it would upset them. The rest of the day he acted like nothing had happened. He told me I was overreacting when I tried to explain how worried I had been.

I apologised to him.

He would often check my phone and read my messages. He downloaded and presented me with a list of the calls I had made and accused me of having an affair with a workmate. I promised not to speak with friends and colleagues again. I immediately shut down my social media accounts to stop him walking out. I was terrified that he would leave me – something he had done before.

I apologised to him.

He returned from gym one morning feeling great and suggested that I do a workout too. For some reason I had a bad feeling about going. But he became irritated and complained that I was never happy with his ideas and that everything always had to be my way.

I apologised and told him that I would only be gone for an hour. On my way home I called to ask if he needed anything from the shops. He didn't answer. My stomach churned and I felt sick.

I arrived home to find that he and the children were not there. I tried to call again. He sent a text saying that if I loved them I wouldn't have gone to the gym. Then he turned his phone off.

I slumped to the floor sobbing, then quickly tried to stop because I knew how much it annoyed him if I ever shed a tear. He used to say that crying was a woman's way of making a man feel bad. But I could not stop the gut-wrenching, overwhelming rage. I was finally aware how little say I had over my own existence and the life of my children who I was desperately trying to protect from his type of 'love'.

Helpless and frantic, I grabbed handfuls of my own hair and pulled as hard as I could. I bashed my fists on the tiled floor in the middle of the kitchen but it didn't help the desperation of not knowing where my children were. I was livid with myself for leaving them and so desperately guilty for going to the gym that I punched myself in my face and head over and over again. I had to punish myself for being such a bad mother and wife. I was at my lowest point but I made myself stop crying, believing that I actually deserved so much worse. In the mirror I was surprised to notice that my face was swollen and bruised already.

When he eventually came home with the kids, he acted normally and ignored my pleas for an explanation. I told him that I had accidentally bumped myself in the head with a weight at gym.

I apologised to him.

***

When we met, I thought he was amazing. He was energetic and good-looking. He was intelligent and gentle, but he also had a cheeky side and would light-heartedly tease me to make me laugh. On our first date, he gave me a handwritten love letter and a necklace with a locket engraved with our initials. He was attentive and wanted to see me all the time.

Even though I was smitten and he showered me with gifts, I often felt an imbalance – that I loved him more than he did me. I tried to talk to him about our relationship, but he told me that if I couldn't feel his love, then it proved that I was the one who didn't care. Each time, I felt guilty, and apologised to him.

Over time, I became an expert at shrinking my thoughts, emotions and beliefs into a picture that he found appealing and acceptable. When he was happy, our life functioned well. When he found a reason to be unhappy with me or felt as if he was being questioned or challenged, he would shut me down, talk over me, disregard my thoughts as being stupid or wrong and withhold his love and affection.

Unconsciously, I tiptoed on eggshells to keep the peace, to keep him happy. I did whatever I needed to stop him from walking out. I never cried or showed anger or frustration as these were the emotions that annoyed him the most. I kept my wits about me, stayed calm and bit down hard to cope. It was such a gradual process that I didn't recognise it was happening. I lost my identity and was merely a reflection of who he wanted me to be.

No matter how good I got at pleasing him, how good a wife I was, how good a mother I became, it was never enough. His goalposts kept changing.

I told him about a new gym that a friend was opening. I said I'd like to give it a try, but he told me it was too expensive for our income, the training methods were a waste of time and that I should know better. 'Just do your morning jogs which don't cost us any money,' he said.

Two months later he told me I'd have to watch my spending because he had joined that gym. I'd have to find another time to jog because he'd signed up for classes at times when I usually ran. He rejected any attempts I made to discuss it, saying that it was typical that I never supported him.

I overlooked his various forms of abuse and narcissistic manipulation. I juggled to pay the bills, but he bought what he wanted at will and berated me for overspending. Our schedule was always his schedule – what suited him and when. I was left to organise our lives around his changing whims and often needed to alter plans at the last moment, so he wouldn't get irritated.

I asked his permission for every social occasion before agreeing to invitations. Many times I pulled out of events at the last minute or came home earlier than planned because I knew he'd be annoyed waiting at home. Embarrassed, I had to then think of excuses to tell people. I felt guilty if I did anything without him, but I excused the fact that he did whatever he wanted to, whenever he wanted to.

Even on the rare occasion when I mustered a scrap of courage to stand up for myself, he would find a way to take back control. One night he told me he was no longer in love with me and there was another woman. Devastated, I left to stay at a hotel.

Two sleepless nights later, after endless texts from him,

blaming me for his affair, he rang telling me that he had taken a pile of tablets and wanted to die. I leapt in the car and sped home immediately, terrified of what I might discover when I got there. I ran inside to find him calmly sitting on the lounge. He admitted that he was fine, he hadn't taken those pills, but he was missing me and wanted me to come back home.

I apologised to him.

***

I worked hard to change, to be a better wife for him. I lived through his subtle isolation of me from family and friends and a few rare cases of physical violence and intimidation. I endured his gradual disintegration of my confidence. I stayed because he made me believe that any problems we had were imagined – or worse, were my fault because he loved me too much to hurt me. I lived through it and I always apologised.

I was exhausted with figuring out how to handle every situation to keep the peace and avoid his criticism or rejection. Luckily, because of the people I worked with, I loved my job and work was the place where I was happy and felt successful. There were many days where my colleagues would see my tiredness and do little things like make me a coffee or bring me lunch and, most importantly, make me laugh.

However, his narcissistic streak attempted to destroy that as well. He would read the kind words that colleagues or clients wrote me in their end of year cards, scoff and cruelly say that they only said those things because they were scared of my temper in the workplace.

It was at a staff meeting, as I watched a presentation by two family violence liaison officers, that I froze in my seat. As they spoke about unhealthy relationships, it suddenly hit me that I was living in a domestic violence situation. I was that person: always on high alert thinking ahead to what could happen in our marriage. I couldn't see the abuse for what it was, until that day when those officers became my smoke alarm.

A warning had been sounded, but it took considerable time for me to really recognise that the smell of smoke always means fire.

After many years of living like this, I ashamedly and tearfully rang an interstate friend and spoke about what had been happening. That conversation was a turning point for me. She challenged me to be honest with myself, asking if I felt enough love for him to stay. Then she asked if I felt enough love *from* him to stay.

She suggested I make an appointment with a counsellor and if he wouldn't agree to go with me, to go on my own. For my sanity, she encouraged me to change my privacy and notification settings on my phone so he couldn't track my every move. Her last point was for me to open a separate bank account and to start depositing a little bit of cash every so often. I was racked with guilt and paralysed with fear, until she quietly said, 'Would you be happy for your children to grow up to have a marriage like yours?'

***

One sunny morning as I played with the kids, my phone buzzed. 'Hope you're ok … thinking of you babe' flashed onto my screen from a woman I knew. My breath caught in my throat and I felt like I was going to be sick. That text wasn't meant for me. My hands shook as I realised it was from his mistress to him, but it had somehow been sent to me as well. His affair couldn't be dismissed any longer. Nor could I ignore that I had married an abusive, manipulative, cheating and controlling man.

After 20 years, I finally worked up the courage to leave our marriage and start a new life for myself and our two beautiful, impressionable children. It was the most difficult thing I have ever done as he made me believe that I couldn't make a decision without his consent.

We separated that day, alternating the care of the kids. When it was my week to move out, I stayed with my mum in her spare bedroom. Thankfully, I had her full support, love and care, which I desperately needed through the heartbreak of being forced apart from my children. The support of my family and workmates was incredibly important before I left my ex, and this magnified even more once we had split up.

There were many days where I sat in the car and shed frustrated tears before I walked into work. But I was an expert at shaking off the bad feelings, painting a smile on my face and 'faking it until making it' each day. I focused on others and their needs and developed a strong empathy and a high emotional intelligence.

To get through the grief, I read whatever I could get my hands on about overcoming manipulative relationships. I trawled through the stages of heartbreak and understood that I needed to retrain my brain. I learned everything I could about narcissistic control, the damage it has on its targets and methods to combat this. I learned that I could get through incredible heartbreak and difficulty. I was terrified of being a bad mother, of living life on my own, but I stood up and found a way to do it anyway.

I increased my exercise. I used it more than ever as a way to relieve stress, find strength and remind myself that I could get through more than I knew. It relieved a lot of anger for me and became a release for the many times when I felt like things were out of control, especially on the days when the children were with him.

Additionally, I started to accept the kindness of others, their compliments and encouragement. Reluctantly at first, I began to allow family and a couple of other significant friends in. I shared parts of my story. I talked about what I was going through and what I had dealt with, and was surprised that I received acceptance and kindness from the people I let in.

Leaning on others was not a sign of weakness, but rather an act of courage. This made others feel important in my life too. I no longer felt shame and secrecy or a need to pretend everything was okay while I shrank into the shadows. This helped with my self-confidence and belief that I am a capable woman who is completely deserving of good things in my life. My daily mantra to myself became, 'I am brave, I am beautiful, I am strong, I am capable and I am worthy.'

A professional counsellor gave me a good insight from someone looking from the outside in. She taught me that I no longer needed to block emotions or hide them. Now I recognise feelings for what they are and allow myself to experience them.

I stopped championing my ex to other people, including our

children. I never spoke negatively about him in any way to the kids and never will. However, I forced myself to stop my ingrained habit of defending him, making excuses for him or hiding the truth. Instead, I found a freedom to become open and transparent about my new life.

Organising the logistics of a marriage split with a controlling man took considerable courage for me. After years of emotional abuse, I had no confidence in my ability to handle legal or financial affairs. However, with little choice but to get on with it, I negotiated with the bank to arrange my finances and engaged a good family lawyer so I knew my rights throughout our separation and divorce.

Any marriage breakdown is incredibly difficult. I feel guilt that I walked away. I miss my children. I will have to live without seeing them for half of their growing years as they spend time between both of our homes. I no longer have a husband to walk the path of life alongside and, strangely, there are times where I feel a deep sadness and regret around this. However overwhelming these feelings may be, this is the flip side: a feeling of incredible relief and happiness.

***

Standing on my balcony, I breathe in the sea air and watch the colours of the water change as the sun sets. My head is clear and free of the once-familiar confusion and fog. This is where I feel safe, content and happy.

I am proud that I stepped up to the task and bought myself a place to live a year after the end of my marriage. I am completely at peace and calm in this space, a feeling I missed out on for over

20 years. I no longer walk on eggshells or live with cruelty or unkindness. I stand tall in my own home.

In less than two years, while forging a new path for myself and my children, I have accomplished so much. I have bought a beautiful new home with water views, and a new car that is reliable and safe. I have achieved many professional successes and enjoyed relaxing holidays. My physical boundaries have been pushed as I've climbed mountains and competed in elite sports events. I feel a different level of confidence and contentment with myself. I know my value more than I ever have and that I deserve so much more than I've had in my life.

I now confidently enjoy a life doing what is right for me and doing right by others. I set healthy limits and boundaries of self-respect. I have genuine friendships – both old and new – with people I would not have been able to spend time with while I was married. Old friendships that were once left crumbling have been mended and I've been brave enough to create new relationships with fun, supportive and loving people.

I have a supportive relationship with a respectful person who gives me renewed hope that there are good men in the world. He has shown me that the way I love is enough and that I am enough.

I feel a calm sense of relief, knowing that I have made the right choice for me and for my children. I can model real love and respect, bravery and strength to my children, showing that mistakes are just that. They are an opportunity to grow and learn, rather than an attack on character and personality.

I sacrificed over 20 years of my life to a cruel, manipulative and unrelenting form of control. In the end, I didn't know who I was.

I understand that others may see me as weak and desperate for staying in such a damaging relationship for so long. There are many who cannot fathom why I didn't just walk away. There have been times when I've asked myself those same questions.

These are the moments when I catch myself and realise that I did nothing wrong. I see things differently nowadays. I know that I am blameless. I was a target for his abuse – not because of my ignorance, gullibility or weakness, but rather, as a result of my positive qualities. I was attractive, confident, caring, easygoing, trusting and hopeful. These qualities were his focus, and I was battered and beaten to boost his ego and make me dependent on him.

Emotional abuse has a long and lingering effect that is impossible to 'just get over' and move on from. I emerge from this each day. I acknowledge that I have been damaged, but that pain no longer controls my life. I accept that I cannot change what I have endured, but I now have a voice to shape a new beginning.

The triumphant moments are the ones where I stop to take in that I am finally free of terror. Every day is infinitely better and full of newfound possibilities. I am living the life I deserve with a freedom to fill it with positivity and love and kindness. I feel stronger, braver and wiser.

My real victory is recognising that letting go of that dysfunctional relationship was not a one-time event. It is something I do every day, over and over again. It is a choice I make for myself and my children, each day.

Without APOLOGY

It is without APOLOGY that I share these steps with you so that you too can begin to let go of that dysfunctional relationship and be finally free from terror.

Without APOLOGY you can be brave, celebrate your beauty, be the strong you and know that you are capable and worthy. Follow these steps to live your life without APOLOGY.

ACTIVITY: Increase your activity. It will help to relieve stress, and it will help you find strength. It is a good reminder that you can get through more than you know. Physical activity can help relieve a lot of anger – it can become a release for the many times when you feel like things are out of control.

PROFESSIONAL COUNSELLING: Seek help from a professional counsellor. They can give you insight from someone looking from the outside in. They can help you to unblock emotions, so you do not have to hide them. This will help you recognise your feelings for what they are and allow yourself to experience them.

OWN MONEY: Open a separate bank account and start depositing a little bit of cash every so often, so you have your own money – an emergency fund.

LEAN ON SUPPORTIVE FAMILY AND FRIENDS: Leaning on others is not a sign of weakness, but rather an act of courage. Do not feel shame or the need to keep the secret or to pretend everything is okay. Share with trusted family and friends. This will boost your self-confidence and belief that you are a capable person who is completely deserving of good things in life.

ORGANISE YOUR AFFAIRS AS QUICKLY AS POSSIBLE: The logistics of a marriage split, coupled with domestic violence, will require a lot of courage.

GET A GOOD LAWYER: Seek out a good family lawyer who has worked with domestic violence and family, as this is a specialty area. There are different domestic violence laws in each state of Australia and in each country.

YOUR LIFE – LIVE IT!: My daily mantra to myself became, 'I am brave, I am beautiful, I am strong, I am capable and I am worthy.' The two words 'I am' are very powerful. Use them only with positive statements to create your Life Mantra. Accept that you cannot change what you have endured, but you have a voice to shape a new beginning. Live the life you deserve with the freedom to fill it with positivity, love and kindness. You will feel stronger, braver and wiser.

© Broken to Brilliant

CHAPTER SEVEN

THREADS WOVEN THROUGH RELATIONSHIPS

'I learned that it is okay TO BE and not TO DO. That negative thoughts can be self-fulfilling prophecies and so can positive thoughts.'

I SUDDENLY REALISED THE TRAFFIC LIGHT WAS RED. ALARMED, I came to a screeching halt, heart pounding. My grip on the steering wheel was so tight that my knuckles were white. My mind spun out of control, running scenarios, trying to find a way to prevent what was likely to come at me in five minutes' time when I walked through the front door to greet my partner. A car horn blared, dragging me back to the reality of the lights that had turned green, and the waiting cars behind me.

As I parked the car outside our home, I was transported back in time. I realised that the overwhelming fear coursing through my body was the same one I'd felt years earlier, when my previous partner's ex assaulted me and threatened to kill me in our kitchen.

Dread settled in the pit of my stomach. Mouth dry, heart pounding, I unlocked the front door. I braced as I stepped across the threshold, scanning for my partner, praying she had found peace today. I was greeted by the silence of an empty room. Then I heard her footsteps on the back deck. Our beautiful dogs came clambering through the back door to greet me with all their vibrant enthusiasm. I knelt to receive their wagging tails and wet noses, and for a moment my heart cracked with a longing for what had been.

My partner stepped inside with a basket of flowers and veggies. I stood up with a tentative smile and still a glimmer of hope that, maybe, this time it could be different. I said, 'That looks like a lovely bounty from our veggie patch.' Hope faded as I watched her scan me from head to toe. Without looking me in the eye or acknowledging my greeting, she turned her back on me and walked off.

I felt the weariness rise as the tension returned to grip my heart. In that moment, I acknowledged to myself that I didn't feel safe in my own home.

***

There were lots of moments that were explosive, hurtful and despairing but this was the day I realised that I was living out of fear. My resources were all being consumed trying to appease or please my partner based on her mood. All to avoid the onslaught of verbal assault and demands, slamming doors, stonewalling, exclusion and withdrawal of connection. I was living in chronic anxiety.

I was no longer resting in my calm, peaceful, joyous, kind self. I was living with unpredictability and felt adrift in confusion, doubting myself and what I heard. I was in way over my head, drowning in misdirection. A game was being played – one that hadn't occurred to me. I had been subtly herded into self-doubt, criticism and worthlessness. Slowly, all my energy, attention and heart went into trying not to lose the love, joy, laughter and togetherness which was alive in the beginning of the relationship.

My own value system of caring, supporting, understanding, and creating had been used to get me to abandon myself and to exist in service of her agenda. I had become co-dependent without even realising it. My innocence had been co-opted and used skilfully.

I really don't know how consciously she played this game. Over the following months I realised there was nothing I could do to stop it, and that I didn't have the skills to change the course our relationship was on. I learned that I was easy to play because of my need to care, and my strong desire for belonging. I was sacrificing all my other needs like a trade-off.

I had fallen into the trap of paying to get my needs met. She had become the only source for getting these needs met. I had been lured to give up my power of choice and freedom without even realising what I was doing. That was a terrifying place to find myself.

***

As I look back and remember the physical, verbal and psychological abuse, I see it always occurred when I felt I was in my safest place, when I let my guard down, when I was my most vulnerable, when I felt my most free, when I felt my most me.

The abuse and violence always occurred in and around the kitchen. The kitchen is the heart of a home, where you expect to nurture, to share, to support with warmth, caring and kindness your loved ones, family and friends.

This was where I so wanted love to triumph, and yet even as a child it was laced with conflict and pain. Harsh, demeaning words were used like weapons, inflicting pain like a scattergun. My reactions and thoughts about those moments stayed with me and became a thread through my female relationships.

Psychological abuse and emotional neglect escalated during two of my relationships. I encountered verbal and periodic psychological threats, along with financial deception and debt, to isolation and the rewriting of truths with family, friends and authorities.

I had gained skills to protect myself from physical danger, but I was lost on how to deal with emotional and psychological conflict. A lot of personal heartache and pain could have been prevented, had I known how to meet conflict in a life-affirming way without sacrificing my own needs.

I did not recognise the risk signs of abuse and domestic violence, and how it was used to keep us in the drama cycle. There were many signs that I dismissed, overlooked and rationalised away. My abusers had to be always right. They had a need to control everything. They hid their true feelings. There was verbal blaming, shaming, guilting, angry outbursts, belittling remarks, criticising, comparing in negative ways – but all done when no-one else was around. They treated the things that I enjoyed in life as trash. I was threatened with physical harm. There was zero remorse, and I was often blamed for their behaviour.

None of these things made me leave the last or previous relationship. What made me leave was when I was written out of the relationship. I was edited out of their words and conversations, excluded from interactions, before the relationship was even over.

It took the second relationship like this before I saw the whole picture. I was selling myself short and needed to gain the necessary skills to deal with conflict. I also needed to get clear about my own needs and how to respectfully get them met. I would no longer allow others' traumas or lack of knowledge to justify the harm they inflicted.

***

I found myself with no money, three weeks to find a place to live, and the likelihood I would be without transport for work after the move. I inquired into services, but I didn't fit the criteria for most services. Those I did fit required so much hoop-jumping that I would have been sitting on the street waiting on paperwork.

I went into overdrive to find a solution. I asked anybody and everybody I met for ideas and worked around the clock to make it happen in the timeframe.

I tried very hard not to carry forward the emotional and psychological abuse. But denying the abuse and violence perpetuated an internal rage fuelled by so many losses. By leaving, I was losing so much: my family, a sense of belonging, somewhere to call home, my dreams, being a parent and grandparent, being among a group of family and friends.

My life now is quite different from where I was 18 months ago when I was in the thick of the aftermath. Violence had been internalised as a way of living even though I knew in my heart that was not who I was. At the time, I saw no clear path out of that nightmare.

The understanding that grew out of the silence within caught my attention more and more. It became my haven from the torrent of words, images and painful emotions.

As my trust in myself grew, I was led to people, places, and processes that brought healing and hope. Eventually, joy began to return. The darkness became less intense, less often. It lost its power to claim my attention and aliveness. I gained more energy and am now living more from my resilience and wellbeing than my fearful thinking.

I had to learn to meet my inner conflict from a place of fearlessness that could not be touched by hellish thoughts and pain. I realised I was the one fuelling the continued existence of the hellish thoughts. I was giving them power by giving all my attention to fixing, eliminating or changing them.

Bit by bit, I woke up. I began to realise that these inner thoughts and feelings came and went, but I didn't have to give them status greater than the clouds in the sky or leaves floating by in the river. I had reclaimed my power. Even harsh, conflictive thoughts became beautiful when I recognised the opportunities they showed me.

This powerful, aware stillness has become my touchstone and anchor. It is always here when I get caught up in a mental or emotional storm, as occasionally I do – especially as I step into new experiences to grow and cultivate a more wonderful life.

***

I would not have been able to undertake all this learning without **support** from friends. Some provided me with accommodation and patience while I found my financial feet. A friend who relocated interstate gifted me her little car, which meant I could keep working. A friend still invites me over weekly to join her for dinner as we engage in our 'abuse free zone' discussions of our successes and share creative inspiration for future projects. Another friend lent me money, so I could buy a vehicle and take advantage of growing opportunities at work.

***

I decided to dedicate a lot of my time to learning. I was willing to do whatever it took to create and sustain healthy, life-serving relationships that make life more wonderful.

My **lifelong learning** has involved things as easy as watching educational videos on YouTube Red. This is a subscription service for advert-free, downloadable videos – inspirational, educational, health, music and how-to videos. This vast resource has fuelled my recovery. I really enjoy listening to Michael Neill and Mary Schiller. I initially found Michael Neill via his book *The Space Within* and Mary Schiller via her book *To Love is to Listen*. Mary Schiller's personal triumph of moving on from a domestic violence history was inspirational.

I also used free online resources to help me understand the nature of violence, and the effect on one's psychology and biology.

Another form of education is reading. I have read lots of books to help me with my recovery. One was on attachment theory. It discusses that attachment styles initially come from our upbringing, but are also influenced by a variety of factors including life experiences. The take-home message was that relationships should not be left to chance. We rely on science for everything from what we eat to how long we exercise, yet most of us know very little about the science behind intimate relationships. They are the most rewarding of human experiences.

Through all my learnings, I discovered that my feelings reflect the thoughts to which I give importance and attention. Feelings are not caused by our circumstances or by others. Circumstances are a stimulus or trigger for the thought or feeling. It is simple really: thoughts become feelings; feelings become actions; actions lead to your results. These results will reinforce your thoughts and create mental, emotional and physical habits.

Become **aware** of what thoughts you give importance and ongoing attention to, because over time your predictive brain will seek to validate the habitual thought patterns. I supported myself in becoming aware and freeing myself from the toxic, violent, hurtful, disempowering, shaming, guilting, angry, blaming, criticising, trivialising, habitual thinking, by doing daily Mindfulness and Open Focus practices. These practices helped me to develop my ability to choose what I pay attention to and to be more flexible in how I pay attention to, and relate to, my inner thoughts and feelings about what is happening.

This has freed up my energy, which was previously caught up in habitual nightmarish thinking. Now I have more energy for making life more wonderful each and every day.

Another thing I did was to use a single word or phrase for what my year was about, and a supporting word each month for action that served that year's word/phrase.

I sing out loud.

I write out a page each morning with **I am nurtured, loved and supported.** I put reminder post-it notes in my lunch box, bullet journal, wallet, and on my phone's home screen. I carry a pocket journal and each day I look for examples of where I am nurtured, loved and supported.

Through the power of awareness, I found 'me' again. The inner nightmare is falling away over time, with mostly sunny days and only occasional storms. I no longer fear my thoughts or feelings. Should I briefly get caught up in the horror movie again, I find I become aware of it when I feel the pain in my body. Then I realise I am being called to attend to my needs in this moment, and life becomes more wonderful.

Some **affirmations to acknowledge, accept and appreciate who I am,** and to experience thoughts that resonate with my essential nature and human needs, include:

- I am nurtured, loved and supported
- I am resilient
- I am creative
- I am powerful
- I am intelligent
- I am kind.

As my mindscape cleared, my confidence shone through. I began to have my own ideas on things, and recognise my needs – but not to the exclusion of others who have a different opinion or method. I began to be able to stand by my own needs and ideas, rather than sacrificing them to avoid conflict or feelings of fear, shame and guilt. Also, I began to realise that I prefer to live in the moment and do so in a creative and celebrative way. I explore possibilities. I try to improve things to run harmoniously and effectively. I work on creating conversations that are deep and honest, that are filled with kindness and care.

Relaxation and restoration of my mind and body was very important. I needed time with myself; quiet time not thinking. I learned that it is okay TO BE and not TO DO. I used to be a normal person, but felt that I no longer was, due to the resulting trauma from that last relationship and its psychological impact.

To move forward, I retrained my brain's neural pathways through meditation, to strengthen the soothing aspects of my biology. I learned about relaxation. I used music to help me sleep and to retrain the brain patterning – like fitness training for the brain.

To restore my body, I changed my nutrition and included prebiotic and probiotic fermented products, whole foods, and supplements to reduce the impact of stress and to facilitate my body's repair.

Other ways I would relax included catching up with a friend from work. We would share a drink together while we laughed loudly, watching comedy shows on TV, or went camping for the weekend on farms to relax in space and nature. I took trips with hiking groups occasionally in national parks, where someone else took care of the details. I connected and restored my creative energy by attending workshops on meetup.com. I hung out with a bunch of women who loved learning.

I used apps on my phone to remember to do things that impacted my finances, health or social connections. These are important details.

***

Connecting and genuineness is a primary need of mine. It is important to me to be able to give my feelings and needs a language, and to meet others with a peace-based language. So, I began to learn nourishing language and non-violent ways of relating through **Nonviolent Communication** (NVC), a simple four-step process developed in 1964 by psychologist Marshall Rosenberg PhD.

The four steps are:

1. describing actions and words that we OBSERVE have stimulated our feelings
2. describing how we FEEL in relation to what we observed
3. identifying our universal human NEEDS that inspire us to take action
4. making a REQUEST for a concrete action in order to enrich our lives.

At an NVC workshop with presenter Kristin Masters, I saw the distinction of how language can be used in a violent way that diminished a person's aliveness or in a non-violent way that supports and celebrates our aliveness and our humanness. This workshop was also where I saw how to meet my own 'inner violence' with empathy and understanding. My use of 'violent communication' was my tragic request for trying to get my needs met. As a result of this workshop, all my emotions got put on an equal footing and could be met in a useful, honouring way and contribute to making my life more wonderful. It showed me a powerfully effective and loving way to relate to others who are in emotional pain.

I have been learning to relate in a healthier way to my own internalised 'violent thinking'. By using NVC, I don't have to sacrifice myself for the good of the family. I can speak up and say there is another way, even if I don't know what it is in the moment.

The **Three Principles** were discovered in 1973 by Sydney Banks, an ordinary working man, who experienced a spontaneous and profound spiritual awakening. He became a world-renowned teacher, author and guide to innovators in such fields as psychology, psychiatry, education, business and even physics, sharing these foundational principles. He uncovered three foundational principles:

1. CONSCIOUSNESS – the gift of awareness
2. MIND – the energy and intelligence of all life
3. THOUGHT – transforms the pure energy of Mind into ideas and images.

Together, these three elements are the golden threads from which all human experience is woven. Outside events and people who I thought caused my ongoing pain are, in fact, not the source of my happiness or distress.

Happiness has become not something I earn, but what I am.

Living with abuse through each life stage has given me a 'syllabus' in the suffering of physical, emotional, psychological and financial abuse. I was eager to share NVC and the Three Principles with others, but I realised I had a way to go before I could do so. For now, I am just focusing on being a non-violent communicator. I am learning a language that resonates with my heart and soul, and that embodies peace and its expression.

Since breaking free I feel blessed as I take a moment to look back over the last 18 months, and see how far I have come in reclaiming my wellbeing, and discovering and shaping a new life chapter. Along with a newly-blooming vegetable patch, a growing creative business, and nurturing new and old friendships. I have left the bitter Winter storms behind, and am embracing Spring and its bounty.

I have LEARNT to be triumphant

Real change is continuing to happen within me and I notice my relating with others is shifting also. This is a joyous moment. Life really has became worth living again, what I have **LEARNT** makes me feel TRIUMPHANT.

LIFELONG LEARNING: Take the time and invest in lifelong learning for your future. This is the way you begin to understand yourself, others, the world and your place in it. Learning is the key to achieving your potential, whatever that may be.

EDUCATIONAL MATERIAL AND RESOURCES: Download apps, read books, listen to audio books when driving, listen to healing music when sleeping. Hook into the power of YouTube and, when you can afford it, get a YouTube Red subscription as this has no advertising. This is a vast resource for healing and recovery.

AWARENESS PRACTICES: Many of us have negative thoughts which affect our confidence, mood and outlook on life. Just as these negative thoughts can be self-fulfilling prophecies so can positive thoughts. Simple awareness practices – mindfulness, Open Focus and affirmations – helped to strengthen my ability to attend to what was important to me, and nurture a more relaxed and clear mind where fresh thinking could arise. With these practices and the Three Principles I no longer fear my own thoughts and feelings. They have  become a rich resource to help me be aware of my needs and find healthy ways to satisfy my universal human needs, both within myself and with others.

Relaxation and restoration: Choose activities that you find relaxing. Go and learn how to relax and meditate from a local centre near you or use YouTube. Activities could include good company, creative outlets, walking in nature. Review your eating patterns. Eat nourishing food and take supplements to help restore your body. Seek professional support from a health professional.

Nonviolent communication: This is a simple, effective and learnable four-step process that allows you to be heard and have the other person feel heard in a shared experience and process of understanding. Watch YouTube videos and attend training. If we all learned how to communicate in a non-violent way, we would have more connected relationships and there would be less violence in the world.

Three principles: Together, these three elements – Mind, Consciousness and Thought – are the golden threads from which all human experience is woven. They helped me understand that happiness doesn't come from outside, but from within.

© Broken to Brilliant

CHAPTER EIGHT

BOUNDARIES, BALANCE AND PRIORITIES

*'We escaped. Every day is a little bit better.
We are thriving and enjoying our freedom.'*

I THOUGHT I KNEW HIM. OUR LARGE AND EXTENDED FAMILIES had lived in the same small country town for four generations. I had schooled and socialised with his siblings. We officially met at a friend's dinner party, and fell too quickly into pregnancy and marriage.

Fast-forward seven years, and I am being held in a stranglehold up against the bathroom wall. He is squeezing my neck with his enormous, rough, man's hands, for what seems like several minutes. I still do not know why this happened. His angry, red, perspiring face is pushed up against mine, and he is shouting as he tightens his grip and I gasp to breathe.

The poor little children are all standing beside me and silently watching as their father strangles their mother. They are very scared, and stand still, unable to do anything.

These choking episodes happened at least three times and became stronger and more vigorous each time.

At around the same time period, I suffered a slow brain bleed, resulting in a massive brain haemorrhage. I was seriously ill for several days and underwent invasive brain surgery to stop the bleeding. The neurosurgeon was puzzled. He couldn't find an aneurysm or any other vascular problem that might have caused this major bleed. 'Have you had a fall? Perhaps a hard knock on the back of the head?' I told him I could not remember anything like that happening.

Recently, I was reading a domestic violence article on social media about the possible side effects of strangling and choking the victim. This article suggested that strangling can cause bleeding in the brain. It has shocked and alarmed me that his choking actions may have been the cause of my life-threatening brain bleed – and that this had not occurred to me at the traumatic time.

***

The verbal and emotional abuse began quite slowly when I became pregnant for the first time. Most days held a hint of his displeasure.

Most things that I did were not quite good enough, and definitely not up to his standards. He started making derogatory comments and insinuations about my appearance. I was too fat, too blonde, had bad breath, my family was crazy, my friends were awful, I couldn't cook properly. Everything that I did displeased him. His permanent scowl and look of distaste did terrible things to my self-esteem and confidence. I started to believe what he was saying to me.

As the kids grew older, his verbal and emotional abuse became louder and angrier, and a lot more regular. It seemed like he was always angry. I realised that the kids and I were walking on eggshells whenever he was at home. We would be very careful of what we said when he was around, and avoid doing anything we thought may upset him. We were constantly on alert.

Whenever I tried to discuss separating, or even to ask if we could attend marriage counselling, he would angrily insist that the children must always stay with him, and that he would insist on 100% custody.

I really felt like there was no good solution to this problem, so I stayed and handled the abuse. He was away with his work quite often, and we enjoyed those times when it was just the kids and me in our home.

He got worse with each passing year. He contributed nothing to the responsibilities of the house, or to the activities of the children. I did everything at home.

I worked full-time. The kids' school and sports were all my responsibility. I did the grocery shopping, cooking, cleaning and all home and kid duties. He did absolutely nothing. If I dared to ask for help, he would shout loudly and verbally abuse me about being a whinger. So, I stopped asking him for help.

He would examine my grocery bills when I arrived home. I would do the shopping and as I was unloading the car he would criticise whatever I had purchased. When I replied that we had several active, healthy kids he would say, 'Well we don't have to feed them all the good stuff,' as he slammed the bill onto the kitchen bench with his fist.

Fortunately I enjoyed my work, but if I came home at the end of the day in a happy and confident mood, he would act quickly to bring me down. He could completely change my mood in five minutes with his negative talk, belittling comments, ridicule and escalating anger. He really didn't like it if I was happy and often would keep it going until I was in tears.

We were married for 14 years. For ten of those years, I wanted to separate and leave the marriage. The safety of the kids was my only reason for staying. I saw myself acting as a buffer zone between him and the poor children. I always had a strong gut feeling not to leave the kids alone with him. They were visibly scared of him. The emotional effect of his constant anger, yelling and unexplainable bouts of 'the silent treatment' was becoming more evident. One child restarted bedwetting for no apparent reason. This went on for several years during primary school. Another developed severe eczema all over the body, even on the face and eyelids. They all had anxiety and were starting to have problems at school with learning and concentration difficulties. One was put into a slow learning class, and with no other reason to explain the cause there was a suggestion of dyslexia.

Their father was becoming less pleasant every day. He would regularly give all of us the silent treatment and was visibly fuming and angry for no apparent reason. He would often ignore us completely at meal times, including special dinners and family parties. We were all blaming ourselves for something we must have done, but we never knew what it was. Sometimes it could go on for hours, even days. We lived in a state of heightened stress all the time he was around. He would refuse to spend any recreational time with us, and we started to take holidays and weekends away on our own.

As most of our 'stuff' happened behind closed doors, to the world, we looked like a normal family at school and sporting functions. Most people, friends and family, were under the impression that we were a happy and harmonious couple.

As time went on, the belittling, confidence destroying, and constant anger increased.

There were times when he would not sleep in our bed. He would say that I wasn't attractive, and he didn't want to be with me. He would go upstairs to sleep in the kids' bedrooms.

Sometime after we separated, I found out that he was abusing the kids.

***

One day, he told me that he was leaving. This was a major relief. He had already arranged a nearby house to live in. He wanted the kids to come to this house for one day and one night most weekends. I found out later that he had three poor women on the go, and that he was in the process of deciding which one was going to be his next victim.

I took the kids interstate to visit family while he packed and organised his move. I thought this would be easier for the children than watching their father prepare to leave our family home. When we returned, he was gone, and the house was very quiet. It took several days to get used to the silence. It was a relief that there were now no arguments or yelling in our home.

I realised over the following weeks that he had taken all of the kids' baby photos and videos with him, any hidden cash and several pieces of my jewellery. Anything that was irreplaceable had been taken during his move.

The first few weeks of our new living arrangements were simple. He went away for a few weeks with his work, and we didn't hear from him. It was bliss. The silence was wonderful. When he returned, the kids started to go to his new house from time to time. They were not happy about doing these overnight stays and asked me several times if they could stay at home instead and just talk to him over the phone. I didn't know then that he was abusing them.

Gradually, the separation turned into a court case. We owned properties together and there was a substantial mortgage in our joint names. I heard on the grapevine that one of his new victims was asking around if anyone knew how much he was actually worth financially, and whether he was worth pursuing. I realised then that it was time to reorganise our finances and officially divorce.

This is when our real problems began to surface. Our time in court was another chapter of shocking, disgraceful abuse by the system. At one stage the children were told they would be living with their father. One child threatened suicide as a result.

After the children disclosed their abuse and refused to go to their father's home, they were taken from me on the spot and became immediate wards of the state. I was called several slanderous and shocking names and accused of brainwashing the children against their father.

He had been telling family and friends that I was mentally unstable. That he had had to leave and separate from me because I had been crazy and very disturbed since the brain haemorrhage and brain surgery. He blamed the marriage breakdown on my 'mental problems'. At the same time, he was making sexual advances and insinuations to my sister and mother. I realise now that he was trying to destroy any support I had.

The court case went on for months, and I was never given the opportunity to tell my side of the story. After months of fighting the system the children eventually came back to live with me full-time. The order was that the children were able to contact him 'at their own request'. They have never requested that contact and have refused to speak to him for years.

Finally, we settled our court case and the divorce was granted. The process of separating and divorcing had been another major chapter of abuse with absolutely no boundaries. There is no logic in those courtrooms. The professionals are not accountable and it was obvious that the case had been planned by more than one party with the aim of causing as much damage as they could to punish me for disclosing the abuse of the perpetrator.

***

When our new chapter started, the children and I were all very damaged and very raw. We had been through hell. I realise now that we were shell-shocked and emotionally numb after attacks at every level. We were together again in our own home, and so we started to rebuild and gain some balance in our lives.

Our **first priority** was our **safety**. We knew by now that anything can happen, and we needed to be aware of our surroundings. He hunted us down and tried to shut us up for years. Due to this stalking, we have moved multiple times to get away from his contact and we are finally stable and loving our new life. We are able to walk and speak freely with no criticism and no harassment and no stalking.

Our **second priority** was our **health**: mental, physical and emotional. As a family, we started to eat healthy food and go walking again. We started to have counselling sessions as we all had anxiety, and were all suffering post-traumatic stress disorder (PTSD) with panic attacks. I was on antidepressants for several years.

Our **third priority** was to **rest and sleep**. We went to bed early and rested regularly. The children were still having regular nightmares. He doesn't know where we are now, so we can sleep peacefully.

Our next project was to buy a dog and it was the kids' choice. We travelled into the country to buy a lovely young pup that they had found online. He was a beautiful pup and has been very adored. This was one of the best decisions we made. My son has told me recently that our pup 'saved his mental health' during these traumatic and emotionally draining times. Our dog has taught and received unconditional 24/7 love from that day. He is still a very strong and positive influence in our lives, several years later. We are blessed to have him in our home.

During the healing, we travelled and took trips and enjoyed having happy times.

We did regular, strength-building exercise. We went for long walks and bike rides. The kids took up sport and I now do yoga and meditation. If I start to feel a little 'low' coming on, I exercise more. It works every time!

I am now an advocate for domestic violence victims in the court system. I belong to several support groups and private Facebook groups. No-one really understands what we have been through, except other victims.

I had no boundaries. I could not say no to anything. I put no value on myself. I let people treat me like crap. This is slowly but surely changing.

I am beginning a psychology course. My children have blossomed and thrived without him in their lives. They finished high school and graduated with outstanding results. They have got into excellent university courses. They have jobs and socialise regularly. They are stable and accomplished young adults.

We escaped, we have moved away. Every day is a little bit better. We are thriving and we are enjoying our freedom. Our life now is very quiet, very calm and mostly smooth sailing. We love our dog, we enjoy everything we do, we enjoy each other's company and we plan our future. I am enjoying work and study. Health and fitness are a priority. We are moving forward in love, light and gratitude. Namaste.

A matter of priorities

It is a matter of setting boundaries, creating balance in your life and setting priorities. The boundaries help to remove disrespectful people and situations from your life. This allows space for the healing to begin. Our main priorities of safety, healthy food, exercise, sleep and rest helped us to restore and rejuvenate. The 'puppy project' restored unconditional love into our home and hearts – it also saved my son. I hope my list will inspire you to set your boundaries, create balance in your life and create your own list of priorities that will help you rebuild your triumphant life.

SET BOUNDARIES: Self-care includes setting boundaries. These are an important part of establishing your identity, necessary for your mental health and wellbeing. Boundaries mean knowing and understanding what your limits are – physical, emotional and spiritual. You need to be in touch with your 'gut' and how you are feeling. When you are feeling frustration, resentment and burnout then you know you have crossed your boundaries and stepped outside of your values. Start small to set better boundaries.

SAFETY: Be aware of your surroundings. Work to keep your new location from being shared. Create a safety plan: have emergency contact numbers listed and a safe place to meet.

HEALTHY FOOD: Eating a healthy, nutritious diet will help restore you physically and emotionally. This means eating fresh healthy foods instead of processed and packaged foods. Every day, eat a varied diet that includes foods from the five food groups:

1. vegetables and legumes/beans

2. fruit

3. lean meats and poultry, fish, eggs, tofu, nuts and seeds, legumes/beans

4. grain (cereal) foods, mostly wholegrain and/or high fibre varieties

5. milk, yoghurt, cheese and/or alternatives, mostly reduced fat.

EXERCISE: Being physically active helps you and your family to have fun again, and to be social. It is essential for your health and wellbeing. Exercise will help give you more energy. It increases your self-confidence and can reduce blood pressure, body fat, total cholesterol and the risk of depression. It is easy and does not have to be expensive – take long walks, do yoga or join community sporting activities.

COUNSELLING: Having someone to talk to, who is there specifically to listen to you talk about your feelings, is invaluable. It can help you feel less alone with your problems and to work on coping strategies. It can help improve your wellbeing and provide insight into how you are responding and reacting to the situation.

SLEEP AND REST: Go to bed early and get plenty of rest. Practice meditation.

Puppy project: Not everyone can have a pet, but if you can, they bring many benefits into your home – the main one being the unconditional love they have for you. Pet owners are less likely to suffer from depression, and owning a pet can help children to develop empathy and learn responsibilities.

Travel together: During the healing, take the time to travel and take small trips to enjoy happy times together in new environments. This can help to release the fear, stress and tension.

© Broken to Brilliant

CHAPTER NINE

DON'T LOOK BACK

'My faith in God and myself kept me going forward and never looking back.'

My very new, very drunk husband came home after a night with his mates and went to sleep. Suddenly in the middle of the night I found myself flying from my bed. Was it a dream? No it had really happened. There I was, sitting on the floor of the van.

'Why did you do that?' I cried.

'Huh? You touched me,' he muttered.

Puzzled and afraid, I thought, 'What do I do now?' I grabbed a blanket and crawled onto the couch, up the other end of the van, and slept the rest of the night sitting up.

I was seven months pregnant. 'Please God, look after my baby.'

***

My world before marriage was very sheltered. I was naïve to the seamy side of life. A child of the fifties era, I had no yardstick with which to judge my violent experiences after marriage.

Our courtship was long distance, so we only saw each other at our best – when we were together on the weekend, once a month. There were also long phone calls, full of love and excitement, but never really getting to know each other.

I did know he had a wild side from some of the stories he told me about his formative years. However, being as naïve and in love as I was, I did not see that it would affect me.

I was married on my 21st birthday as my father had refused his consent for me to marry. (At that time, 21 was the age I could marry without my parents' consent.) My father refused to speak to me until almost a year after we were married. He was a strict, strong-minded man, but fair and loving. I tested him sorely.

Our first home as a married couple was a caravan and we travelled from town to town so he could get work. We would settle for a few months and then move to the next town.

Although I felt scared and often terrified, I never felt hate. But life was to get more difficult and more terrifying.

I have discovered since then that I have two sides to my character which helped me through the bad times. The shy, retiring introvert had the capacity to shut away bad things. The feisty, bold rebel of a teenager – a progressive girl of the sixties – was a capable, strong person.

***

One night, we were off to a party. 'Where are we going?' I said.

'Don't worry, I know the way. It's okay.' It was a very rough road. Suddenly our headlights lit up a car ahead, stopped on the road. Instead of swerving or stopping, he headed straight at it. 'I'm sick of these roads going nowhere!'

Was this another dream? NO – I must act. I grabbed the steering wheel and pulled it left. We went sliding sideways down a bank.

The driver of the other car ran over. 'The road ahead has caved in,' he said. Thank God I was an experienced driver and had been able to steer us away.

I was eight months pregnant and had whiplash. My neck has never quite recovered. I was terrified for my baby and spent the night in hospital recovering and contemplating how I could help the situation. I decided if I was a good, silent wife who would do anything to keep the peace, I could have a happy, safe family life.

***

The terror and the violence never stopped, because his drinking didn't. When I was pregnant with our second child, he threw a toaster at my stomach. Shortly after that he drove off a cliff, but survived unscathed. At that time, I begged my parents to let me come home with my two babies. I was told, 'You made your bed, you lie in it.'

Over the ensuing years, my dread of what was going to happen when he came home after a drinking binge got worse. I never knew what mood he would be in or what would set off the violent beast within.

I was prepared for a lot of yelling, many nasty remarks, and being slapped around occasionally, but I was not prepared for the violence that almost took my life.

The most violent part of my marriage began when my husband was involved in a fatal car accident. He was the only survivor, and was seriously ill for some months. Because he caused the accident, even though he avoided jail time on a technicality it cost us everything. He lost his job and his licence. We lost our home and car, and had to pay exorbitant legal fees.

With help from my parents and friends, I got a part-time job and we moved into an old, rundown house on a very small rent. He eventually got a job labouring.

I had to be strong for all of us as we had many more children by then.

I guess we both had post-traumatic stress disorder. I coped by denial and fantasising. When I could cope no longer, I was prescribed pills such as Valium, Serapax and Mogadon for sleeping. My husband took to drinking more.

I was that doped up I couldn't mother my children properly. My husband became more and more violent. He was throwing chairs, upending the kitchen table and threatening me with knives and guns as well as verbally abusing me. Then he started to knock our eldest around.

***

The night from hell started innocently enough. I went to pick up my baby from my mother-in-law's house after work. My husband was there and I was invited to stay for dinner. Because it was a school night, I declined saying, 'I must get home,' but he stayed.

I organised dinner for the children, followed by bath time and bed. I rang to see if he wanted a lift home, but he was already on his way. He stormed into the house yelling at me for insulting his mother.

'No I didn't,' I said. 'I just wanted to get the kids home to bed.'

Then the red rage took over – the yelling and abuse. My baby started crying so I left the room to calm the little one. I hoped my husband would settle down, but he followed me into the bedroom, picked me up by the neck and pushed me against the wall. I was seeing stars from lack of oxygen, so I started to say the twenty-third psalm. If I was about to die, I needed my prayers.

He asked what was I saying, and I said, 'My prayers.' He threw me on the floor and went to bed.

God had saved me. Now I had to save myself and the kids.

The next morning when I took the kids to their catholic school, I went around to see the nuns – the Sisters of Mercy. 'Please help me.' Remember, this was the 1970s and there was little help for 'domestic matters'.

The nuns took me to my doctor as I had bruises round my neck from the evil person's hands. The doctor phoned the police, who wanted me to bring the kids in to testify against their father. They would not interfere in a domestic matter unless I did so. I said no. I believed it would be too traumatic for the children.

***

Part of me had known my marriage wasn't normal but my problem was that I was brought up to respect marriage. I believed it was forever, so therefore you had to make the best of it. 'You made your bed, you lie in it' was the old saying.

How many signs did I miss in my walk towards self-knowledge? Of course, the obvious answer is that I was blinded by the fact that I was madly in love.

During the 50s and 60s, one didn't really notice what one's parents were doing, as when we weren't at school we were out playing with our friends till dark. My father drank at the local pub and came home and verbally abused my mother. To me, that was a normal part of life, so if my husband yelled at me occasionally, it seemed normal.

My husband's drinking ruled our lives for a long time. His disappearance on a Saturday and his sleeping on a Sunday were how we lived our life.

It was only slowly in the years following the choking incident that I realised that I was married to a stranger whom I loved passionately. I became most unsure about his feelings for me.

***

I had to escape. To escape from a prison, one has to have self-confidence. I had none at the start of our final seven years together.

Planning was the key to success and I had to pull myself together. I stopped all the medication as I realised that I was being treated for my husband's illness. The tranquilisers and sleeping pills would not fix my marriage. I was the one who had to fix our lives.

I am not a person who does things spontaneously. I needed to plan a course of action and, believe it or not, it took me seven years to finally start a new life for me and the kids.

The first building block was getting a job and keeping it. I discovered I was very good at cleaning because of my analytical mind. Order was the key to efficiency and speed.

The next step was befriending the Mercy nuns who taught my children. They offered me counselling and regular prayer sessions – what a godsend they were!

I left my husband for first time after the choking incident, when I went to stay with my parents at the insistence of my boss: 'You have to get away.' I stayed there a month.

My husband came to my work and begged me to go back home. He promised all sorts of wonderful things, and I returned to him. My father was furious, and shortly afterwards he died of a massive heart attack. Now I had to be strong, as I had no-one to turn to for help.

Six months later, nothing in our marriage had changed. In fact it had all become worse.

Even though I had gone back to my husband, it didn't erode the confidence I got from having left in the first place. When Social Security brought in a deserted wives pension, with my part-time job it meant we could survive without him. Suddenly, I had a way out, so I packed the house and kids and moved to another area.

Unfortunately, I was hospitalised for major surgery and was very ill for a couple of months. My husband talked me into taking him back again. As soon as I was well again I went back to my old job and was offered a cooking position as well as the cleaning job.

By this time my husband and I didn't really like each other. We had grown apart. My husband started having an affair and someone told me about it. I had immersed myself in being a good mother and ignored all the signs of my disintegrating marriage. But although my husband's affair was the final catalyst, I had been planning on leaving long before that time.

My self-confidence had been growing thanks to regular prayer and caring friends. We lived in a nice, comfortable suburban house. I was near people. This helped me feel safer, and the kids were able to walk to school.

Then the light-bulb moment came. Here I was, a working mother, with lots of kids, running a household and managing a four-day-a-week job. I was standing in my garden at that time and remember feeling a sense of freedom. I could plan our escape as I now had the strength of purpose to do it.

Learning to balance work and home life helped me become more organised and purposeful. I went from a childlike person with no responsibilities to being an adult woman who knew who she was and how far she could go. I learnt many things, such as how to handle money, how to be patient, and how to be a good mother and wife.

I finally left my husband for the last time and moved myself and the children many hundreds of miles away. Planning our escape was meticulous. A family friend hired a truck. The kids and I packed up the house and left while my husband was at work. I took us hundreds of miles away to start a new life.

The spark of rebellion I had suppressed all those years finally ignited and, this time, there was no going back.

***

Though much more confident by this time, I was still not a whole person. The support of some friends helped me during that time.

I got a job cleaning and waitressing, and began our new life.

I had a friend who was a single father and I helped him look after his children. Lots of kids, lots of headaches, but it seemed to work. However life's lessons had not finished with me yet. My friend became very ill. His children went to their mother and I ended up in a caravan.

I had a good, responsible job, and life moved on. After several more years of cooking, my coordination was off. After many tests, it was discovered that I had irreversible injuries to my neck. Probable cause: the choking incident.

I was given a choice: go on an invalid pension or do some rehabilitation. I chose the latter and the government rehab scheme took me on.

Vocational guidance tested me and suggested a university course. I was on the move upward again, choosing to battle through. This was helpful in many ways. They created opportunities for me to get grief counselling and also provided me with a course in relaxation techniques as well as extra tutoring.

I completed a return-to-study course and was subsequently accepted into university. I completed a bachelor's degree, a graduate diploma, and gained two Certificate IVs. To understand the business world, I worked several years in temping jobs and then finally gained a permanent position. I worked ten years in that job, gaining four promotions in four years. I salted away my retirement fund, living cheaply while adding extra to my super fund.

***

I am now a contented retiree living in my own home. I have many friends through my church and am on several voluntary committees. I have a lovely companion animal, and a beautiful family who have grown to be strong, well-adjusted adults, who own their own homes, have honest professions and beautiful children.

My ex-husband and I come together with the children for their special occasions such as weddings, christenings and special birthdays. If I had hated and been bitter, it would have affected my kids, so I have tried hard over the years to keep up a good relationship with the man.

I still love my husband and understand about his addiction, as do my children. I hoped and prayed that he would fight through his addiction, but he never did.

Facing personal trials and crises makes you stronger, but loving other people instead of yourself keeps you sane. Being aware of your surroundings makes you careful. Just don't look back.

It took a long time to work through the nightmares. Healing my lack of self-esteem and finding my true self took longer, but never giving in to hate helped me move forward.

I don't regret marrying the man and having his children. My love for my children, and showing them how to love, compensated for the fear, dread and terror I experienced on the journey.

***

The day I received my bachelor's degree at the age of 50+ and threw my mortarboard in the air was my greatest triumph. I realised that I did it on my own and that I owned that moment.

One week before I graduated, I still had people saying to me, 'Why did you go through all that at your age?'

I chose a vivid red dress to complement the university colours. I ordered a photographer, checked on family attendance and booked a big table at a local restaurant.

I went to the venue, met all my university friends, and got lost trying to find my way to get my hat and gown. Whoops! Panic stations!

I was with a group who were last into the auditorium. 'So much for my grand entrance,' I thought.

Then my name was called out, and my legs got the wobbles. Luckily, I had friends in front of me and friends behind me. Being handed the piece of paper was like a dream, and the state of euphoria remained even after I got outside. We were all trying to talk at once, young and old alike, until we were herded together for family photos.

Someone yelled, 'Launch the mortarboards!' and we did. As I was throwing mine in the air, I said, 'This is for you, Dad.' I knew this was what he had wanted for me. He saw my potential long before I did. My family was proud of me – my mum just beamed all day. We celebrated well into the evening with champagne and good food.

Most important, I knew that I had the potential to do anything I set my mind to.

Although I went on and pressed ever upwards, I will never forget that feeling of complete freedom. I could have given in to self-pity so many times, but my **faith** in God and myself kept me going forward and never looking back.

Since breaking away from the terror I have succeeded in two new professions and completed three further education courses. I have kept my kids close and encouraged them to do their best. I have kept old friends and found new ones. And, most important to me, I have found peace at last.

Have FAITH

CHECKLIST
☑ _____
☑ _____
☐ _____

TERROR
to Triumph

I felt that God saved me and because of that I worked to save myself and the kids. In God, have **FAITH** that you will get through. This plan of **FAITH** helped me, and it can help you too.

FIND WORK: Get a job and keep it. Having a job can be a crucial factor enabling you to leave a domestic violence situation and relocate to safety. Employment offers those affected by family violence a measure of financial security, independence, confidence and, therefore, safety.

ACTION PLAN: Planning is the key to success. I needed to plan a course of action to start a new life for me and the kids. Plan your escape meticulously for your safety. Keep your plan in a safe place where no-one else will see it. If you have a support person, friend or family member that you can trust, you can share your safety plan with them. Domestic violence services can also help you prepare a safety plan.

Write a list of important and emergency phone numbers, police, general practitioner and children's school. Teach your children how to phone the police in an emergency. Rehearse an escape plan. Pack an emergency bag for you and your children and hide it somewhere safe, like a neighbour's home. Have some emergency cash put aside to assist with your emergency plan. Collect all your important documents and put them in a safe place, including drivers' licence, passports, bank accounts, car registration, housing, insurance and any documents relating to any abuse.

INITIATE COUNSELLING: Grief counselling and/or a course in relaxation techniques or meditation can help heal your confidence and self-esteem. Counselling can provide the emotional support you need such as being listened to, being heard and believed without being judged. It is a safe place to share your story, without fear or shame.

TERTIARY STUDIES: Take a career or vocational guidance test to assist with your future directions. Seek assistance with fees for your studies from scholarships or student loans. Education gives you confidence, financial independence and provides more options for you to create your new life.

HARMONY: Choose harmony rather than bitterness or hate. Never giving in to hate helped me move forward. Harmony helped me and the children, and my family have grown to be strong, well-adjusted adults.

© Broken to Brilliant

CHAPTER TEN

TWO SMALL HANDS

'Empowerment and transition comes from jumping into the fear. Change your life – the journey is yours.'

A DIRTY MESS OF A MAN HOVERED IN THE DOORWAY. HE HAD overheard my phone conversation. Even with my back to him, I could sense his body inflate in the doorway. The space began to narrow. My inner dialogue began to express my nerves. I knew immediately I would have to manage his volatile behaviour and respond effectively if I were to escape the room. I had seconds.

Pretending calmness, I edged under his arm and through the blocked doorway. My defence mechanisms screamed, 'Get me outside!' Almost subconsciously, I grabbed the keys to the car and headed for it, in the garage some distance from the house. I heard my footsteps quicken in the gravel while his screams taunted me. I would not let him see my fear or encourage his pursuit, so I did not run. There was no time to look back. Impending fury was escalating behind me. I told myself, 'Focus, breathe, and get to the car.' Just out of his reach, I scrambled in and locked the car doors.

What was to follow in the next few hours would impact the lives of many.

The glass showed me his clenched fist but kept it from reaching my head. I could almost feel the huff of his hot breath on my neck as it fogged on the closed window. My hairs stood up and his beady eyes rolled back in his head. I was prey, trying to vanish from sight.

'I should slit your parents' throats for having somebody like you!' The words slid down the windowpane and echoed in my ear. Shocked, I couldn't move. The only thing I could think of was to ring my sister and pretend to take photos with my iPhone. Within seconds of holding up the phone I witnessed the evil Hyde turn into the well-mannered Dr Jekyll. Alarmed, I realised he had control of his actions. *What do I do? Where do I go?* Madness had arrived in my home. I could not turn the ignition.

Someone he knew came near the garage, and called out to him. For a moment, his abuse defused. He left. Unseen by all I was left alone – silent and shaken in the darkness of the damp garage.

Our external image projected a great lifestyle. What had just happened? Unpredictable outbursts, then pretending to be functional – this was our pattern. The appearance of devotion and reliability were not real. I tried to calm my nervous system. What would make me happy? I decided to leave the safety of the car and go back to the house to make a costume for my child's school event.

I instinctively locked the door behind me as I entered my home office. I had not realised the hunt was not finished yet. The door clicked. *Thank God I locked it!* There was a pause, then I heard the room's other door slide open – a door I always kept locked! My heart sank.

I was now caught in a room with a madman and his delusions. I could not match his strength. I was pushed up against the wall, feet off the ground. The scissors I'd been using for the costume felt chained to my hand. They were turned on me, forced centimetres from my chest. I couldn't believe my wrist could bend like that. How did it not snap?

These felt like my last moments. I faced a demon in the eyes as he screamed at me, 'I know what I'm going to do: kill you and then myself!'

My mind was racing. I was about to vomit. His malicious intent was now clear. I can't quite describe what happened next – intuition? Something came over me – a power – and my vision could only see white light.

My only defence was effective language. I found a different sound released out of my mouth and a voice that channelled through his haze. 'Who's going to look after our children when we're dead! How will they understand when we're DEAD!'

The words made enough impact for a short physical pause. I became swept up in the wings of spirit and was guided out of there. This time when I made it to the car I did not hesitate, I turned the ignition. The tears streamed down my face as I flew forward down the driveway. I had made a sane choice in an insane situation.

***

Knowing I had a professional person to talk to later that day helped me stay focused. Oh, the irony of having booked an appointment on this day some time ago. I had kept their contact details buried away in my drawer. I'd had no understanding about their service. My assumption was that it was a counselling service we could both go to. As it turns out, the centre was a facility for prevention and education for domestic violence.

My phone rang. 'What! Cancel my appointment? This can't be happening!' They were my only thread of hope. Sweating in my car, I sat in a crowded car park, crying from distress.

They didn't hang up on me. By the end of the call I was assessed as high risk for domestic violence and told to leave immediately. 'Pick up the kids up from school, do not return home, and go to the police.'

'Go to the police? What?' I tried to make sense of the confusion and emptiness. What was happening?

Turmoil flashed before me and I was taken to a memory of trauma 15 years earlier in our relationship. Pushed in the dirt, I had firm hands around my neck with an angry lump of a man on top of me. He was coming down from substance abuse. Both his parents had to pull him off me.

I then came back to the present and the small, soft hands of our children. Eggshell-walking had to stop. My depth of vision expanded. I would no longer devalue my self-worth! I would own knowledge and have power in that. This pattern of abuse was not going to continue for our children. Abusive behaviours were not going to become normalised or permanent.

With only the clothes on our backs and no plans in place, we left. We were cut off from all bank accounts. Our first night was long and exhausting. The car was hidden, the blinds were drawn and then the phone started. One hundred and fifty-one abusive text messages and calls streamed in that night.

***

When you think you love someone, you can blindly give all of yourself away until you are lost. I'm sure his long hours combined with working away made our relationship last longer. Our pattern had become distance, sleep, recovery, followed by reunion, celebration, abuse, and then departure again.

There was a sense of adventure and fun, but what I know now is: it was not real. I did not realise the extent of his dual life, and consequently ours. For nearly two decades, he had a hidden relationship with ice and amphetamines. This was a journey of extreme highs and lows. His mental health deteriorated insidiously.

Life had changed. I pulled my T-shirt sleeves down to hide awkwardly placed imprints that stained my skin all manner of colours – deep blues, greens and purples. I could not explain my situation to anyone. I couldn't tell what was real anymore in our relationship and trust was broken.

It's interesting how I once lived a life continually on a roundabout. Once I was informed about domestic violence, I realised I ticked all the boxes. The more I read the more I could see this was my way of living.

One information pack described my roundabout lifestyle as the Cycle of Violence.
- The Standover Stage – control and fear
- Explosion – self-righteous rage
- The Remorse Stage – justification, minimisation, play down actions and guilt. He was always, always sorry!
- The Pursuit Stage – pursuit and promise, buying back the

partner, helplessness and threats
- The Honeymoon Phase – enmeshment, denial of previous difficulties
- The Build-up Stage – increasing tension.

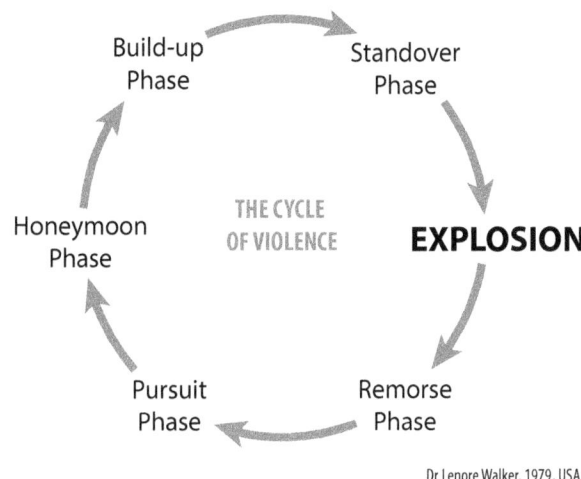

Dr Lenore Walker, 1979, USA

***

I started to make a conscious shift and began to identify my own self-worth. I understood that 'NO.' is a sentence on its own. I would no longer dismiss nasty, suspicious, grandiose, no-shame behaviour or hide the kitchen knives when I washed up. I made a conscious choice to turn off the roundabout, and sped off the first exit.

Hesitantly, I began a tedious life of police, law, breaches and systematic abuse. I was not prepared for this. I had thought the legal system was in place to support good people. My experience was like trying to complete a giant jigsaw without touching the pieces as not one of these services connected. Privacy acts became a hindrance instead of supporting better health recovery. The hunt continued. 'Where's the evidence of this world you state you lived in?' they cried out against me. Mental health can be difficult to measure. People had to listen! I was also left to juggle the wellbeing and financial needs of our children.

In my darkest years I now had to convene legal process. Once, I had to urinate in front of a stranger and pay for drug tests. These were requested by a court lawyer who had never met me or my children. I was patted down, like a criminal. The reason for this testing was based only on the allegations of a diagnosed delusional madman. I would wonder, 'How the hell did I get here?' I thought, 'Next time I go to court I'm going nude because they stripped everything off me.'

The continued psychological abuse was neurotic, crazy and off-topic. The system led us off its true course – 'the wellbeing of the children' – and the perpetrator danced in his allegations in all his glory, seemingly never needing to prove any of it.

My character was defamed. He alleged I had many drug-lord boyfriends and properties overseas, worked as a prostitute and was one of the country's leading computer hackers. Detectives wasted their resources investigating my alleged theft of large amounts of money from him which he had never possessed. In his most extreme delusion, this father believed his children were not his.

What the perpetrator would never understand is a mother's protection for her children is a very powerful energy.

***

It was a hot and humid day when the children's father had a psychotic episode in a suburban street. He held a gun, and was running from and trying to kill someone who was not there. Neighbours went into lockdown and called for help.

Ambulance and police escorted the father to urgent mental health assistance. I knew this day was coming. Why, after two years, had nobody within the system listened to me? Why was I ignored or refused?

What I found most alarming was, this happened on the same day he won a court order to allow him to visit the children without professional supervision. My lived experience is that under the current legal system, the father's right to visitation of his children is placed above examination of his mental health capability.

I was glad I was not afraid to breach this visitation order. Keeping our children safe has always been my first priority. I needed the courts to listen and not miss important information. I wanted them to pay attention to an expert court report containing real concerns about the mental state of the children's father and his self-confessions of substance abuse. I could not wait for a delayed court hearing for this to be reviewed. I was not 'being difficult'. I had to stand up for what was right.

***

The strength of two books has stayed with me throughout this journey.

The first was *A Mother's Story* by domestic violence campaigner Rosie Batty, whose 11-year-old son was killed by his father in 2014 after multiple intervention and custody orders. She demonstrates her personal truth and clearly explains her experiences with misguided process.

The second was a collaborative book, *Broken to Brilliant*, which shared stories of strength and success. My father had heard a broadcast discussing the book on talkback radio. I had to read it; this was what I was looking for. The first night it was delivered, I inhaled the pages and read it from cover to cover. I found new breath. I was no longer alone in trying to understand this madness. The stories of strength and success resonated with me. I started to consider and develop my own identity: *Who am I?*

Some support workers genuinely went beyond their job requirements with their interest and care for me and my children. I was overwhelmed by authentic community members who rallied together and were proactive when needed.

The only time I had returned to my home was under police escort. Time had been limited, and I was only able to grab the bare essentials for myself and the children. The Salvation Army generously supported us with items we needed, food hampers and counselling support. My children witnessed empathy and compassion from people being human in this real-life situation. People gave money, supplied whitegoods and started Go Fund Me pages via Facebook when we were urgently in need of items while the system held hands with the perpetrator. The father would not release items or respond to any of the children's needs while I waited for the courts to catch up.

My friends and family shifted. When surviving trauma, some surprisingly step away and others who you might barely know step up. The unhealthy symbiotic relationship between the children's father and his mother caused her to ignore her grandchildren's cries. The only item of importance for her was to help her son bury the truth.

I noticed there were people I had supported previously who found it uncomfortable to support me in my discomfort. There also appeared to be a social expectation about the recovery timeframe for someone who experiences domestic violence, but that was naïve. My experience is that it is a mental shift that lasts for life.

I have very close and dear friends who walked this journey with me. I was never alone. They are my walking angels who continue to inspire me and hold the flame that keeps the light going.

My parents with their beautiful big hearts gave tirelessly, even while suffering the spreading ripples of trauma themselves. I am proud of the bonds my children have made with them and the resilience they have shared through adverse times. When their father only thought of himself and shirked his responsibilities – it was more important to pay for 'his house' than support the young lives of his children – it was my parents who contributed to the financial needs of their grandchildren. Unconditional positive love and regard pulled us through the struggles, and the greatest gifts were not something that could be bought.

I thought of the many women and children doing this without family support or while living in refuges, and admired their courage. What outstanding strength and skill as they fight for the better good! They need to keep bringing their voices and pounding on doors ignorantly slammed shut until they are heard.

I found talk therapy on its own re-traumatised my experience. I did not want to feel pity or verbalise the experience. I needed strategies. I needed to refine knowledge. There is great freedom not to be blamed for everything and not to be kidnapped from your true life purpose.

For my children there is no more hiding behind the couch or being woken in the middle of the night by their father to see invisible 'people coming to get us'. The father will not call to tell his children he will burn them. Recently my young child made a card for their father on which were drawn love hearts around the word 'Dad'. Curious, I said, 'It's interesting how you have drawn hearts here.' I listened to my child's response: 'Oh, I've drawn them because I have put love hearts around other people's names, I don't want to make Dad angry.' What a different paradigm for a child to think of a parent in this way!

***

What I have learnt about myself is that empowerment and transition can only begin by having the courage to jump into the fear. Embrace the knowledge that fear is trying to teach you, and then move beyond conditioned fears.

From discomfort I peeled through the shell of my old self and found the heartbeat of creativity. I knew I needed to re-skill. I reinvented myself. From my inquiry, destruction was given new life.

Court is still not finalised. A perpetrator uses many delaying tactics and the illusion of law. Justice is caught in old thinking and misses the call of the children.

I felt triumph when we moved from my parents' house. We

lived there for nearly three years. We needed 'our' space. We found shelter among the trees within a great community of people. How was I going to afford this? We found furniture on the side of roads and were given many donations. We made a home. It was safe and loving, a place to rest, sleep and dream.

I pause and notice the wealth in nature. We found nourishment in the gentle shade of the canopy and there was clarity. I hear the birds in flight and I admire their freedom. Look what we have achieved! We began to flourish.

In the beginning I started as a creative person with an easy-going perspective. I embraced adventure, hope and differences. Life was intriguing and full of unexpected directions and colour. My optimism believed the world was abundant.

I am still this person today. My choices are clearer, with boundaries, and full of purpose. This was an opportunity to change my life and activate balance in an unbalanced world. I continue to work with people to right the unique, delicate balance.

I have set up a home of my own that looks out onto nature and nurtures our souls. I am currently studying for my new profession. My children have a strong relationship with their grandparents and I have strong friendships and family connections that continue to support us. The journey continues but we are stronger every day.

I value the gift that everyone has in the freedom of choice in every moment. The journey is mine and yours.

FRAME

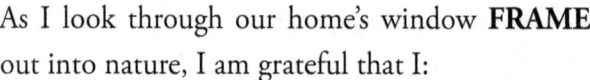

As I look through our home's window **FRAME** out into nature, I am grateful that I:
- had been holding two soft small hands, as this gave me the courage to step into the **fear** of leaving the domestic violence situation
- had the chance to **read** the words from other survivors that breathed hope and inspiration into my soul
- accepted the **assistance** offered from my beautiful, tireless parents and the community, as I too needed my hand held
- **moved** out of the unsafe home to a place of safety
- embraced my **empowerment**.

I hope that as you read this book and my chapter that it will help to FRAME your journey and breath new life into your soul.

FEAR: Have the courage to jump into the fear. Embrace the knowledge that fear is trying to teach you, and then move beyond conditioned fears. We can react to fear in several ways: fight, flight, freeze, friend. In the cycle of violence, all four occur. Leaving – flight – is the hardest. It is also the most dangerous time for you and your family. Prepare a safety plan.

READ: Read books, information pamphlets, brochures and websites about domestic violence. The more I read the more I could see this was my way of living. One information pack described my roundabout lifestyle as the Cycle of Violence. The strength of two books has stayed with me throughout this journey. I recommend *A Mother's Story* by domestic violence campaigner Rosie Batty and a collaborative book, *Broken to Brilliant*, which shared stories of strength and success.

ASSISTANCE: Accept support and assistance from family, friends and services. The Salvation Army can provide support with household items needed, food hampers and counselling support. Allow very close and dear friends to walk the journey with you, so you are never alone – your walking angels, to inspire you and keep the flame alight. My children witnessed empathy and compassion from people being human in this real-life situation. Support from your parents can create bonds with your children, which will help them develop resilience through shared times of adversity. Be prepared that those you thought would provide support may step away, and those you least expected may step forward. There also appeared to be a social expectation about the recovery timeframe for someone who experiences domestic violence, which is naïve. My experience is that it is a mental shift that lasts for life.

MOVE AND MAKE A HOME: Move to a place of safety, with support from police if needed. When you can move to a place that nourishes you, create your own space. Fill it with found-furniture from the sides of roads, and accept donations. Make your home a safe and loving place to rest, sleep and dream. I felt triumph when we moved from my parents' house to our own house.

EMPOWERMENT AND TRANSITION: This comes from jumping into the fear. Change your life – the journey is yours. Being empowered means taking charge of your own life. This involves becoming aware of and moving away from the situation you are in, creating balance, setting boundaries, reading to develop a new mindset, expressing gratitude for all that you have and noticing the wealth of nature.

© Broken to Brilliant

CHAPTER ELEVEN

NIGHTMARES OF MY CHILDHOOD

'Your destiny is yours to create.'

I WOKE UP, PETRIFIED WITH FEAR. I WAS NINE YEARS OLD, ASLEEP in my bed in a lowset house surrounded by forest at the end of a dead-end street. Still in my dream, I instinctively woke, knowing something bad was about to happen. I scrambled out of bed, looked out the window and saw the street filled with crocodiles. They were coming for me. They swarmed through the front door and windows. I tried to find an escape route, but there was no way out. I jumped on a chair and was immediately surrounded by crocodiles.

I woke up sobbing and frightened. No-one knew I had these nightmares.

Except for one night. I must have screamed, because Mum came running in. 'What's wrong?'

'I've just had a nightmare about crocodiles trying to kill me,' I told her.

I couldn't tell her the real reason, because I knew if I did I would never see her again.

***

'Don't tell anyone. This is our little secret, because I love you. If you tell anyone, you'll never see your mother or brothers ever again.' Dad would say, 'It's a man-made law that you can only make love to your wife,' or, 'You're my special little girl.'

I feared night-time because I knew what might happen. It would trigger nightmares so horrifying that I sometimes feared going to sleep. Looking back, I realise the nightmares were representative of what was happening to me – constantly being raped by my dad. This went on for six years.

It would typically go down like this. The family would have dinner, we'd clean up, and us kids would be sent off to bed while Mum and Dad would stay up. They would have a few beers. Mum would fall asleep on the lounge in front of the TV. That's when Dad would come creeping into my room.

Although he didn't hurt me and was always gentle and loving, it made me feel ashamed and dirty – which was so difficult because I didn't really understand why I felt that way. I was so young. I had no-one to talk to, of course. Who would listen, or even believe a little girl? And where would I live if people knew? Besides, no-one would understand how it felt because I was the only person in the world that this was happening to. Or so I thought. It seems so unreal now, like it happened to someone else. Thank God for the healing of time.

Even though I was so young, I often thought life wasn't supposed to feel this sad and lonely. I would sometimes lie in the grassy paddock, looking up into the blue sky, my favourite colour. I watched the clouds form patterns, straining to look further beyond the sky. I would muse about happiness and how that felt, bouncing from one cloud to the next, pondering where the universe ended and what was beyond. The sun and sky always made me feel happy, helping me face another day.

You wouldn't know it now, but I was a shy little girl. I loved music, dancing, playing backyard cricket, riding my pushbike with my trusty dog running alongside me. We lived in a small house that backed onto farmland. Mum and I would ride our horses for hours through the bush. Spending time with my animals was therapeutic. Thank God, I could talk to them, because they understood me.

It wasn't until I was older that the girls at high school would talk about their sexual encounters. This is when I fully understood that what was happening to me wasn't normal, but so wrong. This realisation only made me feel dirtier and more shameful.

There were so many horrible emotions: fear, betrayal, shame, guilt, depression and desperation. In those days, the word 'sex' was never spoken publicly, nor in magazines. There was no such thing as government assistance, nor organisations that helped children. Nor was there any recognition of domestic violence or help for women of any age. The feeling of being trapped and alone never really left me until I was about 42 years old.

I was 13 when I met my best friend at high school. She was the first and only person I felt safe to confide in. It was the hardest thing I had ever done. I was overwhelmed with fear, tears and gratitude. I couldn't believe she believed me. I finally met someone who made me feel safe, and it felt so good. She's still my besty to this day. She's my rock and I know I can tell her anything without judgement.

Most people think I'm happy-go-lucky, but feelings of loneliness and depression sometimes still affect me. I've learned to manage those feelings most of the time, and if I can't, I just tell myself, 'Tomorrow is another day.'

***

The sexual abuse didn't end till I left home at 15.

I had been saving my pocket money over the years, accumulating $800. One day, Dad asked me how much I had and asked to borrow the money. He never paid it back. But I kept working on my escape. I left school at 14, got a full-time job, and secretly squirrelled away enough money for basic household necessities, bond and rent.

When I told my parents I was moving out, my dad was furious.

One night, before I'd finished putting the last mouthful of food in my mouth Dad demanded I get up and do the dishes. I was so over the manipulative moods, I stormed into the kitchen, clanging the dishes with false bravado and attitude, feeling almost empowered knowing I was going to be moving out.

That lasted but a moment. Dad stormed into the kitchen and grabbed me by the throat, his face two inches from mine. Before he could say anything, I slowly, quietly and deliberately told him, 'Never, ever touch me again.' He threw me across the room. I got up, Mum asked me what was going on, and I said, 'Nothing.' Mum always suspected something was up, but my answer never changed. I always thought I'd make a good actress.

That was the last time Dad ever touched me.

Until I moved, you could cut the air with a knife. I found a unit and moved out with a work friend. Dad took the car keys so Mum couldn't help me move. Typical. Nothing was easy in my life unless I was being agreeable, and this became the pattern of my life.

I was finally free – or so I thought.

***

Fast-forward to adulthood. At 17, I met the man who was to become my first husband. We married when I was 20. He was my Peter Pan, rescuing me from my past. I thought marriage meant my life would turn into a romance novel.

Funny how you think a piece of paper will make things better.

It didn't make things better either time. Over the following 25 years, I married two completely different men. Both relationships were filled with abuse.

I was always anxious and fearful of upsetting my partners. I feared being told it was my fault, being threatened with, 'You know where the door is' or, 'You can leave if you don't like it.' So, I did everything I could to try to make them happy. I thought, if I could make them happy and fulfil their needs, they would love me, they would be happy, and they would change.

The more I did the worse things got. I didn't realise that my lack of self-worth and respect perpetuated the problems, creating bigger problems. Instead of gaining respect and love, I was helping my partners become bigger monsters.

All I ever wanted was to be happy and loved in a normal relationship in a normal way. I knew it was possible and tried really hard to make it work. I just didn't know how to make it work. I didn't know about creating boundaries – it wasn't something I had learnt.

The more I tried to make them happy the more they expected and demanded until I had nothing left to give. Once my emotional, physical, spiritual and financial shell was empty, I finally realised how self-centred they were and how little they cared about my happiness. My worthless-o-meter was full.

In both marriages I gained the courage to leave, only to end up going back. I know it's a cliché, but if only I knew then what I know now. Understanding the concept of loving yourself would be a turning point later in my life.

***

In my first marriage, I was terrified what he would do if I told him to his face that I was leaving with his child.

He had a dark side, and would 'take sex' (rape me) because it was his right. He would have had sex three times a day if he could. He was emotionally manipulative. His needs were always met. There was very little to no consideration for my needs. He didn't want me going out with my friends because I might talk to other men. He called me fat during and after my pregnancy. Six months after giving birth, I got my weight down to 49 kg. My father used to call me fat when I was a kid. It made me feel worthless, ugly and unlovable. In my teens, I went through periods of anorexia and bulimia.

He only gave me enough money to buy groceries though I was feeding a newborn and needed to pay for doctors' visits. I thought I was pretty good at stretching the budget. I always tried to buy food he liked. He complained there was never enough food, accusing me of spending it on something else. The rare time he went grocery shopping with me, he would spend three times the amount on food.

Six months after our child was born, he realised that he couldn't afford to support us, so I got a part-time job. But the rules got tighter and tighter. I was constantly stressed and anxious. I felt trapped, desperately sad and lonely. I remember thinking that life could only get better. I was always hopeful.

One day, I made the decision to leave. I knew it was the right decision because it felt right in my gut. I felt a sense of release and freedom. There was a glimmer of hope that I could finally live a happy life. Don't get me wrong, I felt scared, but the feeling of excitement drove me. I quietly anticipated the future, looking forward to being alive again.

I found a share house that didn't mind taking in a mother and child, and found a daycare house for my child. I made a plan to leave while he was at work. I left a short note saying I couldn't live with him anymore, packed the car with a couple of bags of clothes, and fled. I juggled three part-time jobs to make ends meet.

At first, my husband didn't know where we lived. Then he spent the next 12 months trying to woo me back, buying me nice things and taking me out, something he'd rarely done before. He promised he'd change if I came back. I believed him, so I returned. After about 3–4 months the abuse crept in again. I resigned myself to the fact that I'd made my bed, so I had to lie in it. That's what was expected in those days.

***

Oops, I did it again. You would think I'd have learned. But no.

When my first marriage eventually ended, I married a second time to a totally different type of man. He was cool. He had long hair and an earring, and rode a motorbike. He was affectionate and liked to have sex occasionally, but wasn't obsessed about it. It wasn't until we got married after going out for ten years that the cracks split right open. I stayed with him another five years. In hindsight, the cracks were there earlier, I just didn't see them.

The old feelings of anxiety, depression and loneliness crept back into my life. I couldn't believe how naïve and blind I was. He withheld affection and sex. He became addicted to alcohol, prescription drugs and gambling, spending money on boy's toys, and wouldn't pay bills. He knew full well that I was responsible for the bills, because they were in my name. He went out until all hours of the night and sometimes wouldn't return until the next day. He played music so loud, the neighbours would complain, even though he knew I couldn't stand loud music. He later admitted to purposely doing things to upset me.

We bought a house together, and I stupidly put the house in both our names – although I got the loan in my name because he had a bad credit rating. I didn't want him feeling like he wasn't a man. After all, we were partners and were starting a life together. Ain't love grand!

There was always a threat that made me feel unsafe and unworthy. If we had a disagreement he would say, 'If you don't like it, you can leave. I don't have a problem. You've got the problem. You need to get help.' The stupid thing is, I believed it was my fault, so I went and got help from a church he was connected to.

In reality, he had done me a favour.

It was through the church's free counselling service that I learned how to unpack the 'onion layers' of emotional baggage I'd carried with me from childhood.

Little did I realise what a complete shipwreck I had become. My child was the only reason I was still holding myself together. The emotional labyrinth that was my life was about to turn a corner to Sunshine Island.

He eventually told me our marriage was over and told me to buy out his half of the house or leave. Of course, I had no money, so he made an offer to buy me out which was reduced each day I didn't agree. I didn't have any bargaining power, so I agreed and got him to sign it and left. Something was better than nothing. It was better than having to live with constant stress and abuse. Of course, I ended up paying bills he wouldn't pay, and all the legal fees of the divorce. The main thing was: I was free.

My journey had many ugly twists. I moved four times in one year. Every time I found a place to live, the owners either decided to sell or wanted to move back in. I learned to travel light and not be attached to 'things'. I took what life threw at me and adapted – with the help of my besty and a couple of friends.

I liken survivors of domestic violence to the SAS.* Like the SAS, they are beyond brave and resilient against all odds. All of them should be awarded the Purple Heart. This book is our Purple Heart.

I live by my favourite saying: 'Your destiny is yours to create'. Throughout the years, I found different coping mechanisms.

From late teens and particularly through my second marriage I turned to alcohol. I drank and slept around a lot when I was single and drank heavily throughout the second half of my second marriage. I was always looking for love and acceptance.

---

*   Special Air Service Regiment of the Australian Army.

At one point, I started a counselling course with the intention of helping other women. Then I realised I wouldn't cope, hearing everyone's sad and horrible stories, day in, day out. However, the course helped me with my own healing journey.

I began my sporadic spiritual journey in my late teens, going through periods of reading spiritual and self-help books. *You Can Heal Your Life* by Louise Hay, *The Five Love Languages* by Gary Chapman and *Men are from Mars, Women are from Venus* by John Gray were excellent books for relationships and great for a giggle.

I had readings from psychics, looking for the silver lining in my future. I had kinesiology, fabulous for unlocking emotional blocks I couldn't work through myself. Another of my favourite things was guided meditation classes, which really helped calm my overactive anxious mind. I was a bit of a stress head.

I learned to manage my depression through daily exercise. I walked my dogs and went dancing. I learned Latin, modern jive and ballroom dancing, which made my heart sing with joy. I practised visualisation and affirmations out loud as well as writing them.

You might think you deserve to be bitter and twisted. What you deserve is to be happy and safe.

What I've learned is that if you don't do the self-healing work, nothing changes. Learning to love, trust and respect yourself, and being selfish (in a way that doesn't hurt others), is the key to changing everything.

I thought deeply about what would make me happy and made a list. I cut out pictures I liked from magazines and focused on those things daily. I still do those things. I've looked back at previous lists and realised I have achieved everything I've ever written, and more. That's a great feeling to see how much I've grown and what I've achieved.

I've always been good at managing money, no matter how little it was. It's taken me a long time, but I've done quite well and now own a small commercial investment property which is positively geared. I did this by saving up a deposit and getting a loan.

What I did and still do is: work out how much per year each bill costs (electricity, rent, phone, food, petrol) and divide it by 52 weeks in the year. For example, if electricity costs about $1,500/year, divide that by 52 is $26.92. I round that up and save $30/week in the electricity jar. It wasn't unusual for me to only allow $20 a week for myself for clothes or entertainment. Any money left over I saved, even if it was only $10.

I got paid weekly, so that's what I would put into each jar. This took the stress out of managing the bills because I knew the money was always there. Once I got a full-time job, I used the 'salary sacrifice' option to catch up on my super. I feel much safer about my future now.

Never ever leave your financial future in the hands of anyone else. It feels so good when you're financially independent. You know that you will always be okay.

One of my favourite things to do was and is to spend time in nature – bushwalking or going to the beach to body surf and squish my toes in the sand. Time spent outdoors in nature is extremely therapeutic.

After moving four times in one year, I finally found a home

in a better location. This was when I began reflecting on my life and the two abusive relationships. I knew something had to change if I was to have the normal stable, loving, caring relationship and the life I'd always wanted.

I was determined to actively change my mindset. My life began changing from that moment.

I decided that it was not healthy to think about all the attributes I didn't want in a partner, which is what I normally did. I wrote down what I really wanted, no matter how unrealistic it seemed. I wrote how great I'd feel, how I would live, the holidays I'd love to have, the qualities of my ideal man – someone who'd love me unconditionally and make me feel safe. It was my wish list.

Every morning, I affirmed out loud what I wanted, visualising what that looked and felt like.

My life did a complete turnaround.

Within 12 months, a couple of years after my second marriage break-up, my vision became reality. I met my current partner who I have been with for 12 years. He truly cares about my happiness, loves me unconditionally, empowers and supports me.

When someone truly loves and cares for your happiness, you can tell them anything and it makes you closer and stronger together. Don't get me wrong, it's not all roses. It's still a journey you go through together. That's what a loving relationship is all about.

BRAVES

What I've learned is if you don't do the self-healing work, nothing changes. Learning to love, trust and respect yourself is the key to changing everything.

'BRAVES' is a list of my coping strategies from my healing journey. This is my purple heart to you.

BOOKS: Read self-help and spiritual books.

RECOGNISE: Learn to recognise the signs and red flags of abuse such as: expecting you to spend all your time with him, blaming alcohol or drugs for his behaviour, acting possessively, playing mind games, making you feel guilty. Also recognise you need to heal the unhealthy patterns in yourself and work on that. That is when real, positive change starts.

AFFIRMATIONS: Change your mindset. Write your affirmations and read them aloud. Only write and speak aloud positive words. That's what you will attract back.

VISION BOARD: Think deeply about what would make you happy. Make a list. Cut out pictures from magazines and glue them onto a piece of card to make a vision board. Focus on your vision board daily.

EXERCISE: Exercise your mind and body daily. Walk the dog, meditate, spend time outside in nature – go bushwalking or spend time at the beach, body surfing and squishing your toes in the sand. Daily exposure to the sun produces 'feel good' endorphins beneficial for your mental health.

Savings: To get ahead, start saving money, a minimum of 10% or more of your income. Make it a habit and it will build up for your future.

CHAPTER TWELVE

TO THE ONE WHO LOVED AND HURT ME

Love always protects, always trusts, always hopes, always perseveres. (1 Corinthians 13:7)

ON THE NIGHT OF MY GRADUATION CEREMONY, YOU JUMPED ON me at the afterparty.

I was flattened on my back and ground into the asphalt. My shoulder, hip and leg were injured. In the taxi home I held a hanky to the blood on my shoulder and asked you, 'Why? What had I done?' You said you didn't know why.

It left a scar.

Deeper than the flesh wound, that incident left a mental scar that was to freeze my life for years to come. The whispers in my head said: *Don't bother trying to meet your dreams. They will be ground down.* I was ground down, knocked down ... but I always got back up.

The scar on my shoulder came to represent one of my lowest points. All my life I had wanted to join my chosen profession, and the legacy of that attack on me still leaves me confused. How could you say you loved me, and then be so cruel? Crueller still, how could you deny ever hurting me? You used to say it was my fault: 'If you hadn't made me aggro…'

I am sorry I made you angry. I am sorry you hurt me.

***

I remember it all … the push-shove walk home from the club as you twisted my arms behind my back, bruising my wrists. Releasing me, letting me run behind the trees then coming after me again.

The black eye when we were working outdoors together that you said I deserved.

The humiliation of having my clothes torn off so I could not leave the house leaves me numb. The time you tore my clothes in front of your parents, is without sense still.

Why did you push me outside onto the step with no clothes on, only underwear, when I was bleeding after an operation?

The pain when my hair was held and my head banged on the carpet so hard that I could feel the cement floor underneath. I begged you to stop before your dad got back from the shop. I cried in the bedroom, and then I covered it up. I felt so ashamed.

The smashing of our furniture, and me tidying up and walking along the driveway under the cover of darkness with broken things to put them out on rubbish night.

Lying in my mum's bed after I caught the bus to her house to rest, and feeling the sting of the carpet burns and the tenderness of the bruises on my arms. The time I took refuge at a co-worker's house after another incident. The time your friend's girlfriend noticed the bruises on my legs.

The secrets I kept about the soft-tissue damage in my back. Going to work with bruises on my legs and backside.

The beers that you poured over me to humiliate me. The smoke that you blew in my face, drunkenly taunting me. You broke me down. I felt less than human – devalued and degraded.

Holding our baby while you drove drunk and angry. I thought you would kill us. Feeling ashamed that I had postnatal depression. Feeling isolated. And still your heavy drinking continued, even after the baby.

Ringing me to pick up the kids after you had hurt our eldest in front of our youngest and left them out on the verandah in their pyjamas.

Being pushed and shoved up those concrete stairs as you held my head between your hands and forced me to look upwards at the stars.

Living a life of guilt, responsibility and shame. Always being the designated driver.

Coming to terms with the emotional reality of the abuse. Juggling my working life and then coming home to detached routines. It was exhausting and lonely.

Heart pain and anxiety attacks. I drove myself to hospital in a daze.

***

Flashback

The kitchen waltz
did not have a rhythm
of harmony or grace
as I beheld the fury
your red-eyed, cornered grip
fixed upon your face.

The muscle ripple of your arm
your poisonous words
the alcoholic vapour.

No escape
no escape
to friend or foe or neighbour.

Trapped tense, back snapped
against the bedroom wall.

Shaking cold with fear
Shh. The children sleep so near.

Talk calm, talk down
reassure, placate, disarm
walk slow across the kitchen floor.

A shower sob, a locked-door cry
you hurt me
and I want to die.

Dress, dry, arrange
place you soft in bed
check the kids
and kiss their heads.

Sleep beside you
say, 'It's all right'
plot to leave throughout the night.

You snore in peace.

From this nightmare
I dream of my release.

***

I developed a belief that you were my rock and that if you said, 'Everything will be all right,' then it would be, even after another incident of cruelty and abuse. It was part of the crazy-making. The man who hurt me in so many ways claimed he loved me and wanted to protect me.

Over many years I believed your promises of a new life. You would say, 'I am your family.' We had such tender times, and then the abuse would corrode trust and happiness. Each new betrayal was a broken promise – about not hurting me, about treating me better, about reviewing the alcohol. It broke my heart, and the cracks had a pattern. The words 'I love you', 'I'm sorry', and 'It'll be all right' were the mortar you rendered over our flawed marriage.

I did so love you.

I didn't understand until I heard the words from the counsellor: 'This man has not got your best interests at heart.' That day, the illusion shattered irreparably.

And she was right. After everything I had been through with you, it was undeniable.

The truth emerged, not the half lies and distorted 'truth' you hid your abuse behind, but the cold, hard reality. That painful truth set me free.

You were in the room with me. You would remember it, because you hadn't been drinking that day.

You were still privately abusing the kids. Their counsellor

validated what was not visible in public. The children and I were acknowledged to be victims of domestic violence. Your attempts to deny your abuse of us added to our stress and pain. You showed no remorse – only blame and accusations.

***

One night after I asked you not to give beer to a teenager at a BBQ, you cornered me in the kitchen and assaulted me. The children were asleep. I left our house in my nightie to go to the police station. You followed me, pulled me by the wrist, pushed and shoved me up the stairs. I paid that night for running away. I was sure our neighbours must have heard, but no-one said anything.

Three days later I rang a work colleague and finally 'told someone'. My back and shoulder were injured. You paid for the physiotherapist – thank you. Just like you would later help the kids and I move house – fear was mixed with gratitude.

I resigned from that job, unable to return. I became socially withdrawn and started to experience panic attacks.

It was part of the 'learnt shame' that I was somehow to blame. Falling apart with the stress of the abuse was another burden I had to carry in loneliness.

I hardly recognised myself with the anger and grief. All those years had taken their toll and the safety valve had blown. There were times that I morphed into the same traits I despised. I was controlling, enraging and demanding. The years of abuse had taken their toll. I had been silenced. Speaking out was a desperate plea for help. I was fighting for my survival. I did not want to be engaged in this conflict but my defences and boundaries had been eroded. It left you with plenty of ammunition to say: 'Look at what she has done.'

The focus was shifted to my behaviour.

Pointed out that it was undignified for a woman to be acting so raw.

Did you really have no empathy?

No real understanding of the emotional torture and physical pain I had endured over the years?

***

It took me over 20 years to finally leave you. I left the year we met, the years I was engaged, the first year I was married and many, many times afterwards, including – bizarrely – post-divorce, after we reunited because you said we had an 'unconventional marriage'.

I tried so hard to mother and work in a situation that swung between affection and abuse. By the time I was living with PTSD my light had nearly gone out and darkness crept in.

The final blow of infidelity sounded the death knell to the secret 'us'. I had been through this before but this time it hit the hardest. I imploded in a desperate scramble, unable to cope. Left alone amid the fallout I searched for the guts of who I was and could only find unrecognisable shreds.

I couldn't make sense of your senseless pursuit of me, then your betrayal. I couldn't, and at times didn't, make sense to myself and to others. To others we were a loving couple, and even, post-divorce, amicable … but that was not the full reality.

I clung to you, mourned the loss of our family home and begged for answers that you couldn't give. What followed was a slow annihilation of my sense of belonging.

The mixture of deceit and betrayal were too much for me or the façade to handle, and it all shattered. It became evident in the supermarket or social settings that the lie of my life was written all over my face. I became a walking ghost. It was clear I was altered. I was hardly recognisable, even to myself. It wasn't just my paleness, my thinness, and my dizziness from being in intense pain. I was in a daze from being betrayed. None of my kindness, forgiveness of past injuries or love of you seemed to count for anything. It was like I had been dropped into a foreign country with the wrong currency and I couldn't provide for my basic needs.

I remember asking you for the money you had promised me to do Christmas shopping for the kids. You said, 'You'll get it when you start behaving yourself.'

By that time I was falling apart, and not behaving as myself.

I had constant stress and fatigue from the abuse that you decreed as 'ancient history'. I thought I had known what it took to rebuild a life – I had repacked boxes and suitcases many times and waited till bruises faded and memories were filed under 'secret'.

But the events I was to experience left me stripped and stranded in the wasteland that was once my personal and professional life in a way that I had never experienced before. I lost all bearings. I lost myself, I lost hope, I lost trust, I lost my confidence, I lost my clarity of thought, I lost control of my emotions. I became hostile, angry and confused. The years of crazy-making had affected my behaviour.

I was required to write a deposition and an inventory of the abuse. The memories brought a great sadness. I had always been confused as to the love I felt for you and your behaviour towards me.

***

In war the first casualty is said to be truth. I watched you rewrite my experiences until 25 years later, after years and years of loving you, I was reduced to a nervy 'unreliable witness' because I could not remember my son's birthday. I was traumatised. In the court, your solicitor had a 'take no prisoners' approach. It was as if I was reliving the abuse.

When the façade cracked, the secondary social backlash became a new source of grief.

The silence and stares from people in our community, people who knew me from work, and others that knew me as your wife, were like a second blow. I could not cauterise the pain, the shame and the humiliation. No-one seemed to be able to equate the man they 'knew' from the truth that had begun to leak out from the rubble of our relationship. No-one could believe this good, kind, friendly man could hurt anyone.

When the story broke through the silence and shame, you pointed blame at me. 'You have waged war against me,' you said. My nerves were shot.

After I had retaliated during that final incident, you said you were the victim and I was the perpetrator. That was my lowest point. You were now slandering me and distorting the truth out of context. Some of your friends were my friends. Some were the family members of my clients. These were community-minded people who participated in White Ribbon rallies to end domestic violence – as did you.

You distorted reality so that my experiences were not validated. It was hard to stay in that town. I was having flashbacks and my anxiety was high. I was now a broken, angry woman. You had turned the tables and presented yourself as a victim. Without the facts of the whole picture, rather than the pieces you had presented, and without sighting court and medical documents my abuse was minimised and denied.

I know the truth because I lived it. A later apology from the senior detective helped, but it came too late. The damage was done.

The tears were endless, the pain was excruciating, like a death, and the result was, in every way, like a death of me – at least my former self.

I cried often and had an edgy irritability and an uncontrollable jumpiness. Flashbacks taunted me, triggered by a sound or a smell or a feeling. Memories I had buried deep while surviving it all were washed ashore in the final year of grief and confusion.

In the end I was diagnosed with Post Traumatic Stress from the abuse you minimised as 'ancient history'.

The psychologist said: 'My impression is that at this time, the situation is best understood in the context of a long abusive relationship and a recent separation with ongoing problems with her ex-husband attempting to intimidate her.' I wasn't diagnosed with major depression or bipolar disorder. 'She will need to be monitored for emergence of post traumatic stress disorder in the longer term.'

I was finally named a victim of crime, based on legal aid paperwork and medical records recorded across three states over 25 years.

***

Building a new life wasn't easy. The backlash from you and my community was intense – almost as painful as the initial abuse. I had to begin to heal from both.

Far away in time and space from your abuse, I was walking on the beach one day and it crept up on me. I felt a deep sense of peace. My health and happiness were on the upward road. I felt more myself than I had in years. I had rebuilt a new life.

To the One Who Needs Hope

Hope anchors the soul. (Hebrews 6:19)

If there is one quality that I know guided me through the debris of my former life, it is Hope. Hope is the bridge to a triumphant life. Hold onto it.

'Recovery' implies 'redemption'. 'Healed' implies 'no longer wounded'. The 'post' in PTSD implies that the past is processed and placed in a context that gives meaning to one's life.

This is not true all the time, but sometimes it is. I no longer move through life with the intensity of feelings and trauma that altered my thoughts and my breathing. I am no longer numb with disbelief or exhaustion from trying to make sense out of crazy-making.

The conclusion I have reached is that you must have hope. Hope redeems the past and guides the present and the future. It is more than platitudes or affirmations, although these things are supportive. It is an act of courage. It is a conviction that even a dark day or month, year or decade will not dim the light of life.

That spark could be different for different people. It could be the babies or children that need you. It could be work, rest, the quiet moments of a bath, the patting of your family pet, the song that lights your spirits and takes you to a place where you remember who you were or were meant to be and are now becoming.

It could be a belief in life or God or both, but not nothing. It has to be something. I call it Hope. It is my foundation for building a life with a sense of peace and purpose. Hope casts out the darkness of the past, shines guiding Light and gifts love and laughter.

Even life is a traumatic event. We are all altered, whether we are the perpetrator or the victim or the bystander. Trauma caused by others, by illness, by suffering – this is the nature of life.

I can't un-carry the past, the abuse, the trauma and the reality. I have tried to outrun it, unpack it and lose it. But whether I'd had these experiences or others, I would still need to carry myself through life with hope, with compassion, with forgiveness.

I just didn't think it would be so heavy. None of us who have experienced domestic violence do. It was almost life-and-soul crushing. I was immobilised by pain and gripped by the fear of fully living. I knew I wanted to be free to experience a full life. I didn't know how. The aftershocks of the abuse left me disorientated. There were times I had to work extremely hard and push myself, and at other times I needed to rest.

The one point of departure from the darkness for me is hope. Hope gives us freedom to stretch our wings.

We can remain caged in our own negative self-thoughts,

treatment and beliefs. These heavy layers dampen our direction. They burden us with self-abuse. It doubles the weight of the injury and clips our self-actualisation.

Self-acceptance lightens the load of constantly needing to be triumphant in our lives. It releases the need for reassurance that we are recovered or worthy enough to slip back into the stream of life. We get to choose who we are. We get to experience reality with clearer eyes. That is our freedom and our reward.

Hope in the middle of struggle strengthens us. I am not sure how it does that, but I know it to be true. We must grieve, because it is painful to have experienced domestic violence. Pain with love is destructive. It has damaged our loved ones and us.

We hope because that is the fundamental tenet of life.

Whatever hope means to you I wish you strength and courage to claim it. Support from others and shared stories and experiences will resonate with you and give you comfort and sound advice, and you will need that at times, but more than that you will need Hope. That is the key to our freedom.

I wish you practical help and emotional empathy with your journey post-abuse in your present life. I wish you courage to float when your will to swim is exhausted. I wish you warm comfort in quiet sacred moments that not even the intense pain of your experiences can freeze. I wish you gentle self-care – therein lies the wisdom and the meaning of healing and self-love.

Hope is our birthright. Claim it and nurture it. Hope is the promise of the phoenix that a new life will rise from the ashes. A new life awaits you.

Since breaking free from the abuse my heart has healed. I

have been loved back into wholeness by my children, family and friends. I have peace in my life and a strong sense of hope. My body, mind and soul continue to heal after enduring beyond what I thought I could.

I have rebuilt my life on foundations of love and forgiveness. I have undertaken university studies and moved to a friendly community. I write children's and young adult stories, as well as poetry. The abuse and brokenness is behind me.

I walk in the gentle and brilliant Light of Triumph that I survived the abuse, that I am a survivor and that I am free.

P.S. I graduate at the end of this year with a Master's degree – this time with no scar.

HOPE

To rebuild your life after abuse you need HOPE.

HEAL: Allow yourself to heal. There were times I had to work extremely hard and push myself, and at other times I needed to rest.

OPTIMISM: Create optimism. Believe that there will come a day when you will no longer move through life with the intensity of feelings and trauma that altered your thoughts and your breathing. You will no longer be numb with disbelief or exhaustion from trying to make sense out of crazy-making. It could be a belief in life or God or both.

PURPOSE: Restore your sense of purpose. It could be the babies or children that need you. It could be studying for new qualifications, or finding a way to help others who have been through similar experiences.

EMOTIONS: Support your emotions. It could be work, rest, the quiet moments of a bath, the patting of your family pet, the song that lights your spirits and takes you to a place where you remember who you were or were meant to be and are now becoming. Support from others and shared stories and experiences that resonate with you and give you comfort and sound advice.

© Broken to Brilliant

GLOSSARY

THE PEOPLE IN THIS BOOK HAVE EXPERIENCED MANY FORMS OF ongoing abuse. This glossary provides definitions for domestic and family violence and the associated behaviours.

Domestic and family violence, also known as domestic violence, family violence, partner violence or intimate partner violence, is a pattern of abusive behaviour between family members and/or intimate partners, usually, though not exclusively, taking place in the home, that over time puts one person in a position of power over another, and causes fear. It is often referred to as a pattern of coercion and control. Abusers are sometimes called 'perpetrators of violence'. [23, 24, 25, 26]

Family and domestic violence is any violent, threatening, coercive or controlling behaviour that occurs in current or past family, domestic or intimate relationships. This includes not only physical injury but direct or indirect threats, sexual assault, emotional and psychological torment, economic control, damage to property, social isolation and any behaviour which causes a person to live in fear or torment.[23, 24, 25, 26]

Types of abusive behaviour associated with domestic and family violence are listed below:
- Physical abuse – including direct assaults on the body (shaking, slapping, pushing), use of weapons, driving dangerously, destruction of property, abuse of pets in front

of family members, assault of children, locking the victim out of the house, and sleep deprivation.
- Sexual abuse – any form of forced sex or sexual degradation, such as sexual activity without consent, causing pain during sex, assaulting genitals, coercive sex without protection against pregnancy or sexually transmitted disease, making the victim perform sexual acts unwillingly, criticising, or using sexually degrading insults.
- Emotional abuse – blaming the victim for all problems in the relationship, constantly comparing the victim with others to undermine self-esteem and self-worth, sporadic sulking, withdrawing all interest and engagement (e.g. weeks of silence), blackmail.
- Domestic violence threats are a form of emotional abuse and are threats made within the context of an abusive relationship. Whether the threats are of a physical, sexual or emotional nature, they are all designed to further control the victim by instilling fear and ensuring compliance.
- Verbal abuse – continual 'put downs' and humiliation, either privately or publicly, with attacks following clear themes that focus on intelligence, sexuality, body image and capacity as a parent and spouse or capable person.
- Social abuse – systematic isolation from family and friends through techniques such as ongoing rudeness to family and friends, moving to locations where the victim knows nobody, and forbidding or physically preventing the victim from going out and meeting people.
- Economic abuse – complete control of all monies, no access

to bank accounts, providing only an inadequate 'allowance', using any wages earned by the victim for household expenses.
- Spiritual abuse – denying access to ceremonies, land or family, preventing religious observance, forcing victims to do things against their beliefs, denigration of cultural background, or using religious teachings or cultural tradition as a reason for violence.

The above behaviours are from Box 1.1: Behaviours associated with domestic and family violence, Office for Women 2008; Inspire Foundation 2008.

ENDNOTES

1 Kosenko, K., & Laboy, J. 2014. 'I survived': The content and forms of survival narratives. *Journal of Loss and Trauma, 19*(6), 497–513. doi:10.1 080/15325024.2013.808948

2 Méndez-Negrete, J. 2013. Expressive creativity: Narrative text and creative cultural expressions as a healing praxis. *Journal of Creativity in Mental Health, 8*(3), 314–325. doi:10.1080/15401383.2013.821934

3 Anderson, K. M., & Hiersteiner, C. 2008. Recovering from childhood sexual abuse: Is a 'storybook ending' possible? *American Journal of Family Therapy, 36*(5), 413–424. doi:10.1080/01926180701804592

4 Franzway, S., Wendt, S., Moulding, N., Zufferey, C., Chung, D., & Elder, A. 2015. *Gendered violence and citizenship: the long term effects of domestic violence on mental health, housing, work and social activity: Preliminary report.* University of South Australia: Magill, SA. Retrieved from http://www.unisa.edu.au/PageFiles/71190/Gendered-Violence-and-Citizenship-report.pdf

5 Loxton D., Dolja-Gore X., Anderson A. E., & Townsend, N. 2017. Intimate partner violence adversely impacts health over 16 years and across generations: A longitudinal cohort study. *PLoS ONE, 12*(6). doi:10.1371/journal.pone.0178138

6 Anderson, K. M., Renner, L. M., & Danis, F. S. 2012. Recovery: Resilience and growth in the aftermath of domestic violence. *Violence Against Women, 18*(11), 1279 –1299. doi:10.1177/1077801212470543

7 Jones, A. & Vetere, A. 2017. 'You just deal with it. You have to when you've got a child': A narrative analysis of mothers' accounts of how they coped, both during an abusive relationship and after leaving. *Clinical Child Psychology and Psychiatry, 22*(1), 74–89. doi:10.1177/1359104515624131

8 National Council to Reduce Violence against Women and their Children. 2009. *Background paper to Time for Action: The National Council's plan for Australia to reduce violence against women and their children, 2009–2021.* p. 13. Viewed 28 October 2010. Retrieved from: https://www.dss.gov.au/our-responsibilities/women/publications-articles/reducing-violence/national-plan-to-reduce-violence-against-women-and-their-children/background-paper-to-time-for-action-the-national-councils-plan-for-

australia-to-reduce-violence-against-women-and-their

9 Tually S., Faulkner D., Cutler C., & Slatter, M. 2008. *Women, domestic and family violence and homelessness: A synthesis report*. Flinders Institute for Housing, Urban and Regional Research: Adelaide, SA. Retrieved from: https://www.dss.gov.au/sites/default/files/documents/05_2012/synthesis_report2008.pdf

10 Victorian Government, Department of Human Services. 2012. *Family violence risk assessment and risk management framework and practice guides 1-3*. (2nd edn.). Retrieved from: https://providers.dhhs.vic.gov.au/sites/dhhsproviders/files/2017-06/family-violence-risk-assessment-risk-management-framework-practice-guides.PDF

11 National Council to Reduce Violence against Women and their Children. 2009. *Background paper to Time for Action: The National Council's plan for Australia to reduce violence against women and their children, 2009–2021*. p. 13. Viewed 28 October 2010. Retrieved from: https://www.dss.gov.au/our-responsibilities/women/publications-articles/reducing-violence/national-plan-to-reduce-violence-against-women-and-their-children/background-paper-to-time-for-action-the-national-councils-plan-for-australia-to-reduce-violence-against-women-and-their

12 Evans, I. 2007. *Battle-scars: Long-term effects of prior domestic violence*. Monash University: Melbourne. Retrieved from: http://www.chilliwebsites.com/sitefiles/553/File/Battlescars.pdf

13 National Council to Reduce Violence against Women and their Children. 2009. *Background paper to Time for Action: The National Council's plan for Australia to reduce violence against women and their children, 2009–2021*. Viewed 28 October 2010. Retrieved from: https://www.dss.gov.au/our-responsibilities/women/publications-articles/reducing-violence/national-plan-to-reduce-violence-against-women-and-their-children/background-paper-to-time-for-action-the-national-councils-plan-for-australia-to-reduce-violence-against-women-and-their

14 Garcia-Moreno, C., Guedes, A., & Knerr, W. 2012. *Understanding and addressing violence against women: Overview*. World Health Organization: Geneva. Retrieved from: WHO/RHR/12.35 http://apps.who.int/iris/bitstream/10665/77433/1/WHO_RHR_12.35_eng.pdf

15 Australian Institute of Health and Welfare. 2018. *Family, domestic and sexual violence in Australia 2018: Report*. Retrieved from: https://www.aihw.gov.au/reports/domestic-violence/family-domestic-sexual-violence-in-australia-2018/contents/table-of-contents

16 KPMG. 2016. *The cost of violence against women and their children in Australia: Final report*. Retrieved from: https://www.dss.gov.au/sites/default/files/documents/08_2016/the_cost_of_violence_against_women_and_their_children_in_australia_-_summary_report_may_2016.pdf

17 Campo, M. 2015. 2015. Children's exposure to domestic and family violence: Key issues and responses. *Child Family Community Australia Information Exchange Paper No. 36*. Retrieved from: https://aifs.gov.au/cfca/sites/default/files/publication-documents/cfca-36-children-exposure-fdv.pdf

18 World Health Organisation. 2000. *Women's mental health: An evidence based review*. World Health Organization: Geneva. Retrieved from: http://www.who.int/mental_health/media/en/67.pdf

19 Evans, I. 2007. *Battle-scars: Long-term effects of prior domestic violence*. Monash University: Melbourne. Retrieved from: http://www.chilliwebsites.com/sitefiles/553/File/Battlescars.pdf

20 Humbert, T. K., Engleman, K., & Miller C. E. 2014. Exploring women's expectations of recovery from intimate partner violence: A phenomenological study. *Occupational Therapy in Mental Health, 30*(4), 358–380. doi:10.1080/0164212X.2014.970062

21 Reid, R. J., Bonomi, A. E., Rivara, F. P., Anderson, M. L., Fishman, P.A., Carrell, D. S., & Thompson, R. S. 2008. Intimate partner violence among men prevalence, chronicity, and health effects. *American Journal of Preventive Medicine, 34*(6), 478–485. doi:10.1016/j.amepre.2008.01.029

22 Coker, A. L., Davis, K. E., Arias, I., Desai, S., Sanderson, M., Brandt, H. M., & Smith, P. H. 2002. Physical and mental health effects of intimate partner violence for men and women. *American Journal of Preventive Medicine*, 23(4), 260–8. doi:10.1016/S0749-3797(02)00514-7.

23 World Health Organization. 2002. *World report on violence and health: Summary*. World Health Organization: Geneva. Retrieved from: http://www.who.int/violence_injury_prevention/violence/world_report/en/summary_en.pdf

24 Women's Council for Domestic and Family Violence Services. 2011. *What is Domestic and Family Violence?* Retrieved from: http://www.womenscouncil.com.au/what-is-domestic--family-violence.html

25 State Government of Victoria, Department of Health & Human Services. 2011. *What is family violence?* Retrieved from: https://services.dhhs.vic.gov.au/what-family-violence

26 Tually S., Faulkner D., Cutler C., & Slatter, M. 2008. *Women, domestic and family violence and homelessness: A synthesis report.* Flinders Institute for Housing, Urban and Regional Research: Adelaide, SA. Retrieved from: https://www.dss.gov.au/sites/default/files/documents/05_2012/synthesis_report2008.pdf

CONTACT NUMBERS

Australia National

- 1800 RESPECT (1800 737 732)
  24 hour, National Sexual Assault, Family & Domestic Violence Counselling Line for any Australian who has experienced, or is at risk of, family and domestic violence and/or sexual assault.
- Lifeline 131 114
  National number that can help put you in contact with a crisis service in your state (24 hours)
- Police or Ambulance 000
  In an emergency for police or ambulance.
- Translating and Interpreting Service 131 450
  Phone to gain access to an interpreter in your own language (free).
- Mensline Australia 1300 789 978
  Supports men and boys who are dealing with family and relationship difficulties.
- Kids Help Line 1800 551 800
  Telephone counselling for children and young people
  Email and web counselling: www.kidshelp.com.au
- Australian Childhood Foundation 1800 381 581
  Counselling for children and young people affected by abuse
  Website: www.childhood.org.au
- Relationships Australia 1300 364 277
  Support groups and counselling on relationships, and for abusive and abused partners.

Website: www.relationships.com.au
- Blue Knot Foundation (Adults Surviving Child Abuse)
  1300 657 380
  A service to adult survivors, their friends and family and the health care professionals who support them.
  Website: www.asca.org.au
- National Disability Abuse and Neglect Hotline
  1800 880 052
  An Australia-wide telephone hotline for reporting abuse and neglect of people with disability.
  Website: www.disabilityhotline.org
- LGBTIQ Domestic Violence Information: Another Closet
  Website: www.anothercloset.com.au
- Qlife 1800 184 527
- Transgender and Transsexual People:
  Gender Centre (02) 9569 2366
  Services for people with gender issues.
  Website: www.gendercentre.org.au
- National Suicide Prevention Lifeline 13 11 14

Australian Capital Territory
- Domestic Violence Crisis Service 02 6280 0900
- Rape Crisis Centre (24 Hours) 02 6247 2525
- Canberra Men's Centre 02 6230 6999
- Legal Aid ACT 1300 654 314

New South Wales
- Domestic Violence Line 1800 65 64 63
  1800 671 442 TTY (Hearing impaired)

- Rape Crisis Service 1800 424 017
- Interrelate Family Centres 1300 473 528
- Legal Aid NSW 1300 888 529

Northern Territory

- Domestic Violence Crisis Line 1800 019 116
- Domestic & Family Violence Centre (YWCA) 08 8932 9155
- Sexual Assault Referral Centre 08 8922 6472
- Northern Territory Legal Aid Commission 1800 019 343

Queensland

- Domestic Violence Telephone Service 1800 811 811
- Sexual Assault Help Line 1800 010 120
- Men's Info Line 1800 600 636
- QLD DV WebLink (a directory of QLD support services) www.qlddomesticviolencelink.org.au
- Legal Aid Queensland 1300 651 188

South Australia

- Domestic Violence Crisis Line 1800 800 098
- Yarrow Place Sexual Assault Service 1800 817 421
- Legal Service Commission 1300 366 424
- MensLine Australia 1300 789 978

Tasmania

- Family Violence Counselling and Support Service 1800 608 122
- Family Violence Response & Referral 1800 633 937

- Sexual Assault Support Service
  03 6231 1817/ 03 6334 2740
- MensLine Australia 1300 789 978
- Legal Aid Tasmania 1300 366 611

Victoria

- Safe steps Family Violence Response Centre
  1800 015 188 or 9322 3555
- Sexual Assault Crisis Line 1800 806 292
- Men's Referral Service 1800 065 973
- Victoria Legal Aid 1300 792 387

Western Australia

- Women's Domestic Violence Helpline
  08 9223 1188/ 1800007 339
- Crisis Care 1800 199 008 or 9233 1111
- Sexual Assault Resource Centre 08 6458 1828 or 1800 199 888
- Men's Helpline 08 9223 1199 or 1800 000 599
- Legal Aid WA 1300 650 579

United States of America

- The National Domestic Hotline 1-800-799-7233 | 1-800-787-3224 (TTY)

United Kingdom

- National Domestic Helpline 0808 2000 247
  24-hour National Domestic Violence Freephone Helpline

Contact details were correct at the time of publication.

ALSO IN THIS SERIES

Broken to Brilliant
Breaking Free to be You After Domestic Violence – Stories of Strength and Success

ISBN: 978-0-9945714-0-3

"That would never happen to me. I'm too strong. I would walk out." Those were KC Andrews' thoughts as a trainee nurse listening to a lecture on domestic violence. But when it happened to her, it took years to finally leave.

She has now rebuilt her life from the ashes of a brutal marriage, and along the way met other women who have survived the fog of fear and feelings of worthlessness – and then on the outside, endured the disbelief and bureaucratic bungles of those who should have helped.

But now, each woman's brilliance is emerging once again.

Each one tells her unique story to help readers understand the many different shapes domestic violence can take. And yet the focus of this book is not on the horror, but the healing. Each woman shares the skills, techniques and attitudes that helped her to shine once again.

This book is for anyone who is living in an abusive relationship, knows someone who is, or has emerged and is looking for a roadmap out of darkness into the light of new beginnings.

Bronze medallist, eLit Book Awards 2017

Broken to Brilliant is an Australian Not For Profit Charity where Domestic Violence Survivors Mentor other Survivors to re-establish successful lives. These courageous women are mothers, accountants, nurses, managers, models, executive managers, sales trainers and account executives. Each at a different stage in re-establishment and recovery, they have banded together to share how they have rebuilt their lives.

www.ingramcontent.com/pod-product-compliance
Lightning Source LLC
Chambersburg PA
CBHW070548010526
44118CB00012B/1261